Contents

Setting the Stage ①

What is Flash?

Flash is known primarily as software used to animate objects and to create multimedia projects. However, although Flash is used for animation, there are actually three distinct areas that Flash is used for:

- Animation
- Vector Graphics
- Interactivity

Animation

In Flash, each animated document you produce is called a **movie**. You can do **frame-by-frame**, **tweened** and **guided** animations using the **Timeline**. All these methods are explored in this book.

Vector Graphics

Did you know that you can actually buy a version of Flash that doesn't have a **Timeline**? This is because Flash is used by many graphic designers simply as a tool for creating vector graphics. The vector graphics capability in Flash was developed because of the need for graphics with small file sizes; vector graphics occupy much less file space than bitmap graphics. For this reason, when you learn Flash, you first need to learn how to create vector shapes. The first part of this book focuses on vector graphics.

Interactivity

By **interactivity** I mean that the Flash movie changes according to user input. The building blocks of interactivity are **buttons** and **ActionScript**; you place a button in your Flash movie, then attach programming code called **ActionScript** to it, which makes something happen when the button is pressed. You can build a whole website using just Flash, with buttons and a lot of **ActionScript**!

This book covers the basics of buttons and **ActionScript** but doesn't go as far as showing how you would put together a whole website. You will learn how to publish your movie and create an HTML file, how to create a small standalone interactive application, and also how to insert a **Flash** movie into a **Dreamweaver** website.

Let's get started!

This chapter will briefly introduce the different parts of the **Flash** workspace.

 Load **Flash**. You can do this in one of two ways:

 Either double-click on the **Flash** icon (if there is one) on your Windows desktop

 Or click **Start, All Programs, Macromedia** and then select **Macromedia Flash MX 2004**.

 Macromedia Flash MX 2004

If **Flash** has never run before on your PC then the **Macromedia Product Activation** window will appear. Follow the on-screen instructions to activate or trial the software, as appropriate.

When **Flash** opens, you should see the **Start Page**, which has a red bar at the top. If you don't see it this just means that when the software was previously used the **Start Page** was switched off.

Tip: To show the red **Start Page**, select **Edit, Preferences** from the **Main Menu** bar. On the **General** tab, set the option **On launch** to **Show Start Page**.

Creating a new document

O   On the **Start Page** choose **Flash Document** under **Create New**.

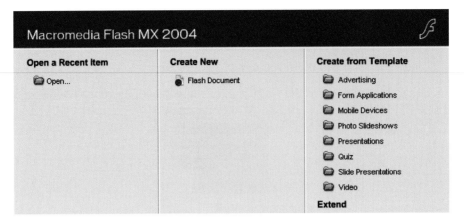

Figure 1.1: The Start Page

Tip: You can also open a new document without using the **Start Page** by selecting **File**, **New** from the **Main Menu** bar, then clicking **OK** in the window that appears.

Your screen will now look something like this. It seems complicated!

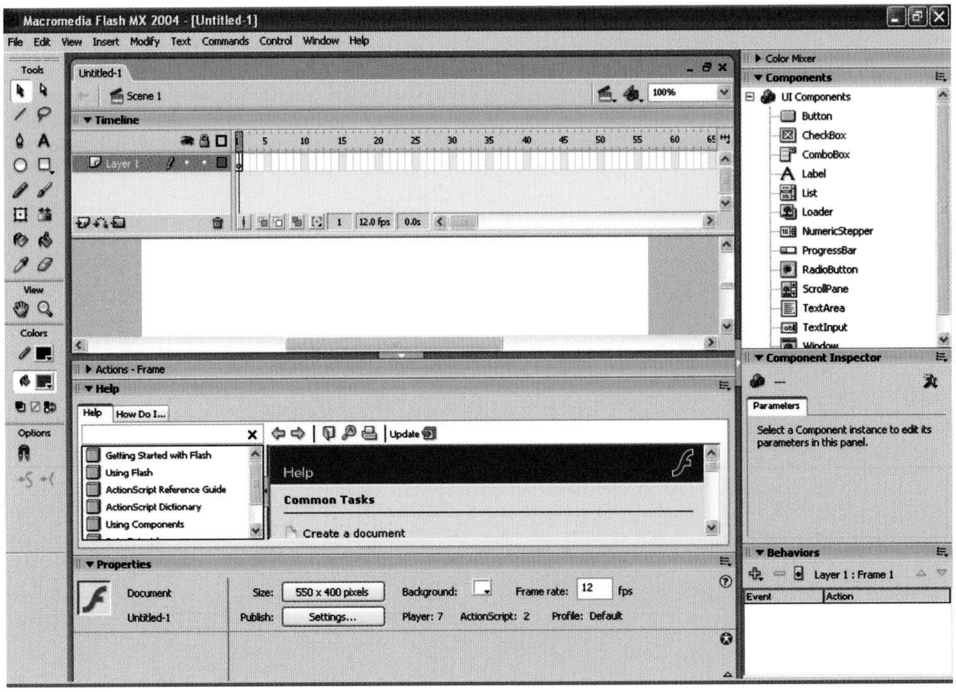

Figure 1.2: The Flash workspace

Panels

The screen looks complicated because there are lots of open **panels**. Panels are a bit like windows in Microsoft applications, but they can cause confusion if you have not come across them before. If you have used **Dreamweaver** you will be used to panels.

Panels are not to be feared! They can be opened, closed, maximised and minimised just like windows.

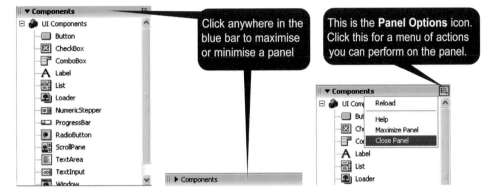

Figure 1.3: Panels

◐   Close the **Components** panel by clicking its **Panel Options** icon then selecting **Close Panel** from the menu that appears.

The panel completely disappears; not even the blue title bar is visible.

Opening a panel

All panels can be opened using the **Window** option on the **Main Menu** bar. Some panels are in the main list, and some are in sub-lists.

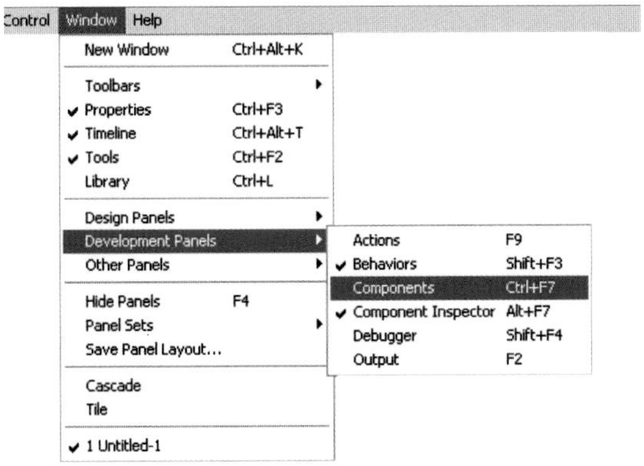

Figure 1.4: Opening panels from the Window menu

◐   Open the **Components** panel by selecting **Window, Development Panels, Components** from the menu.

Minimise panels

Now we'll minimise all the panels to clear up the workspace.

○   Start by minimising the **Properties** panel (click the blue bar at the top of the panel).

○   Now minimise each of the other panels in turn.

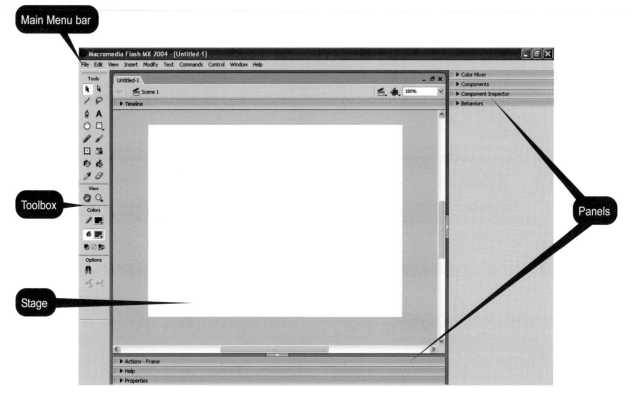

Figure 1.5: Simplified Flash workspace

The large grey area is the **Work Area**, and the white box is the **Stage**. This is where the content for all your animations and graphics will be drawn or imported to. Notice that the **Work Area** resized to fill the space as you minimised the panels.

○   Use the scroll bars to move the white rectangle (the **Stage**) into view.

That looks much better! This is the basic workspace with no panels open. We will open each panel as we need it.

The Toolbox

The **Toolbox** contains all the drawing and text tools, as well as tools for selecting, zooming, and more.

You select a tool by clicking its icon in the **Toolbox**. Some tools have options that control how they work; these are displayed at the bottom of the **Toolbox** and will change according to which tool is currently selected.

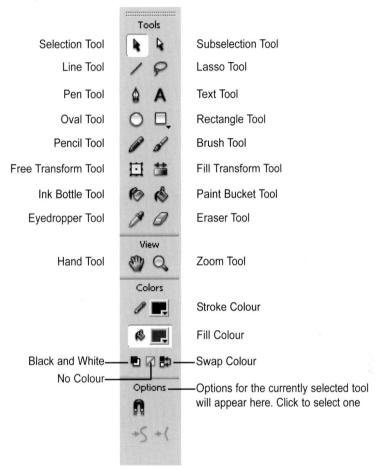

Figure 1.6: The Toolbox

❶ If you want to know the name of any tool, hover the mouse over its icon and a **tool tip** will appear.

The Properties panel

We'll take a quick look at the properties of the **Stage** using the **Properties** panel (also called the **Property inspector**).

 Maximise the **Properties** panel by clicking anywhere in the blue bar at the top of the panel. (If your **Properties** panel isn't visible, select **Window, Properties** from the menu bar.)

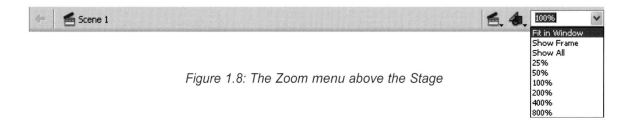

Figure 1.7: The Properties panel

❶ Here you can view and change various properties of the **Stage**, such as the size and the background colour. We'll leave these settings as they are for now.

> **Tip:** The **Properties** panel displays different settings according to what you are doing. If you have a different tool selected in the **Toolbox** you may see different settings. If your Properties panel looks different from the one above, just click the **Selection Tool** icon in the **Toolbox** to display the **Stage** settings.

The Zoom menu

You can choose how large or small to view the **Stage** using the **Zoom** menu, located at the top-right corner above the stage. Click the down arrow and select an option from the list, or type in a percentage. **Fit in Window** is a useful option to get the whole **Stage** into view.

Figure 1.8: The Zoom menu above the Stage

The Zoom tool

If you want to zoom in on a particular part of the **Stage** it's best to use the **Zoom** tool in the **Toolbox**.

 ●   Click the **Zoom** tool in the **Toolbox**.

 ●   At the bottom of the **Toolbox**, select the **Enlarge** tool.

●   You can either click and drag a rectangle around the area you want to zoom in on, or just click once on the area.

> **Tip:** You can hold down the **Alt** key to switch quickly between the **Enlarge** and **Reduce** tools.

●   When you are finished with the **Zoom** tool, click the **Selection** tool in the **Toolbox**.

Saving and Closing

Even though we haven't drawn anything yet we'll save the document so that the **Stage** settings will be saved.

●   Select **File, Save As** from the **Main Menu** bar. Find a suitable place to save the file. Enter **drawing_exercises** as the **File name**. Leave the **File type** as **Flash MX 2004 Document (*.fla)**. Click **Save**.

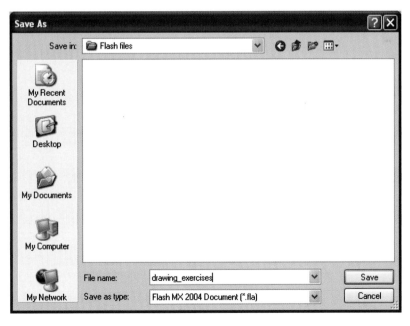

Figure 1.9: Saving a Flash document

●   If this is the end of a session, close this document by selecting **File, Close** from the **Main Menu** bar, and close **Flash** by selecting **File, Exit**.

Simple Vector Graphics

2

One of the things **Flash** is particularly good at is creating vector graphics. Vector graphics consist of lines and shapes defined mathematically, rather than as a collection of coloured pixels. This makes them very easy to select and transform.

We'll create some drawings as a brief introduction to some of the tools in the **Toolbox**.

Opening a document

▶ If your **drawing_exercises.fla** file isn't already open, click it on the **Start Page** if you can see it, otherwise click **Open**, find the file, and click **OK**.

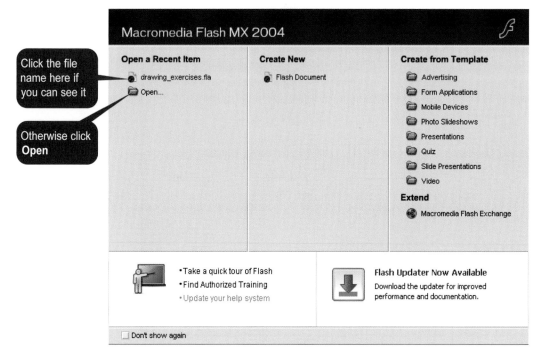

Figure 2.1: The Start Page

The Pencil tool

The **Pencil** tool is a freehand drawing tool; you can use it to draw lines or shapes. It has some extra useful features – **Flash** can turn your wobbly line into a nice smooth curve!

○ Select the **Pencil** tool from the **Toolbox**.

○ At the bottom of the **Toolbox**, click the **Options** icon and select the last option: **Ink**.

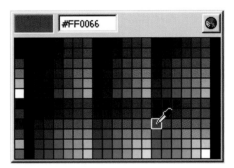

Figure 2.2: Toolbox options for the Pencil tool

○ Expand the **Properties** panel at the bottom of the screen if it is not currently visible. Click the small colour box next to the pencil symbol (the pencil symbol is the **Stroke Color** icon). Click any colour from the palette that appears.

Figure 2.3: The Color palette

○ In the **Properties** panel, change the line width to **2** by clicking on the down arrow and then dragging the slider. Alternatively, just type **2** in the box and press **Enter**.

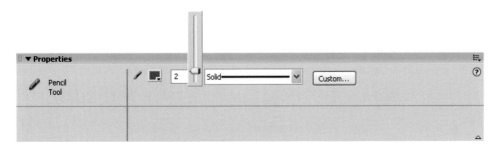

Figure 2.4: The Properties panel for the Pencil tool

○ On the **Stage**, draw a curved line and a straight line. Change the stroke in the **Properties** panel to be a dashed line, then draw a circle.

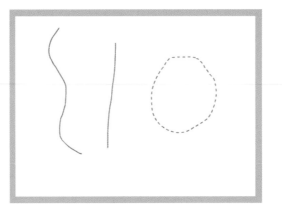

Figure 2.5

The **Ink** option is unassisted – **Flash** makes almost no effort to make your lines look smooth or straight.

The Selection tool

This is probably the tool you will use most often.

○ Click the **Selection** tool at the top of the **Toolbox**.

○ Click on your curved line. It will become thicker and have a dotted mesh on it to show it is selected.

○ Now click on the straight line. The curved line is no longer selected. To select more than one object you must hold down the **Shift** key while you click the objects. Try this now to select both the straight and the curved line.

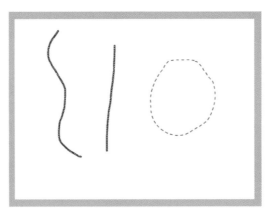

Figure 2.6

Now that both lines are selected, you can move them around the **Stage**.

○   To move an object that is selected, you click and drag it. When the **Selection** tool is over a selected object, the pointer changes to a double-headed arrow. Move the pointer over one of the selected shapes, then click and drag to move both selected lines.

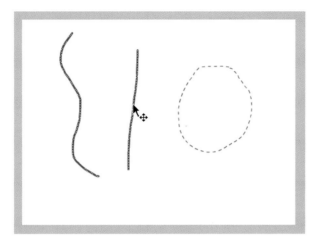

Figure 2.7

○   Now deselect the lines by clicking away from them, on an empty part of the **Stage**.

○   Select the curved line, then look at the bottom of the **Toolbox**.

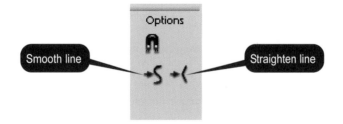

Figure 2.8: Toolbox options

There are options here to smooth out the curve or to make it straighter.

○   Click the **Smooth** icon repeatedly. Notice that your line gets smoother!

○   Now select the straight line and use the **Straighten** icon to make it completely straight.

Using the Selection tool to alter a shape

🔘 Deselect everything by pressing the **Escape** key.

🔘 Without first selecting it, click and drag a part of the curved line.

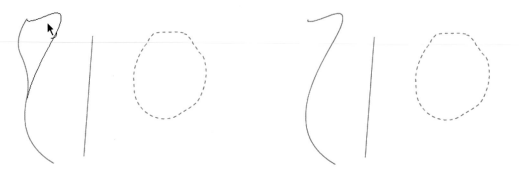

Figure 2.9: Reshaping a line with the Selection tool

The line moves as if you were pulling a piece of string. This can sometimes be very useful, but you need to be careful; when you're trying to move lines, you must select them first, or you will accidentally reshape them.

Selecting using a box

Now we'll select both lines using a different technique.

🔘 Click and drag a box around the two lines on the **Stage** with the **Selection** tool.

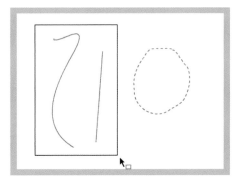

Figure 2.10: Selecting using a selection box

Everything in the box is selected!

❶ Be careful to make sure the lines are completely in the box – if they aren't, the box will cut the lines. We'll try this later.

Deleting objects

🔘 The two lines should now be selected. To delete the lines, press the **Delete** key.

Changing properties of an existing shape

This is very straightforward; you just select the object using the **Selection** tool, then use the **Properties** panel to change anything you like.

- ◉ Use the **Selection** tool to select the circle.

- ◉ In the **Properties** panel, change the stroke back to a solid line.

- ◉ Change the colour of the line using the **Properties** panel.

- ◉ Use the **Straighten** option at the bottom of the **Toolbox** – a couple of clicks should transform it into a perfect circle!

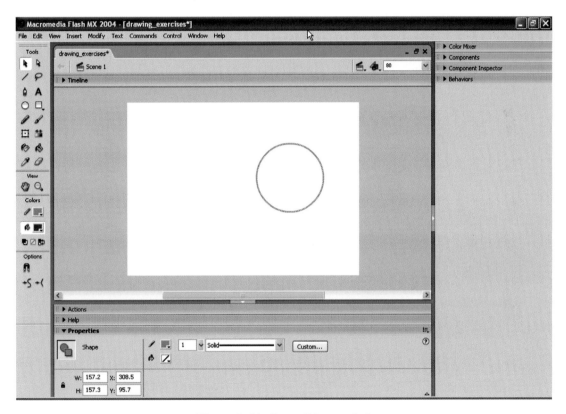

Figure 2.11: Smoothing a circle

The Paint Bucket tool

The **Paint Bucket** tool is used to add a fill to objects that only have a stroke, such as the circle we've drawn.

Tip: The outline of a shape is referred to as the **Stroke**.

 ▶   Select the circle if it isn't already selected.

 ▶   Click the **Paint Bucket** tool in the **Toolbox**.

 ▶   Look at the **Properties** panel.

▼ Properties

	Shape			1 ▾	Solid————————— ▾	Custom...	⑦

W: 157.2   X: 308.5
H: 157.3   Y: 95.7

Figure 2.12: The Properties panel for the currently selected object

The **Properties** panel shows the properties of the currently selected object. So what happens when nothing is selected?

 ▶   Press the **Escape** key to deselect the circle. Now take a look at the **Properties** panel:

If the name of the tool is displayed here, then the **Properties** panel is displaying the properties of the selected tool. If **Shape** is displayed, the properties of the currently selected shape are shown instead.

▼ Properties

Paint Bucket Tool

Figure 2.13: The Properties panel for the Paint Bucket tool

The **Properties** panel has changed. Because nothing is selected, it shows the settings for the currently selected tool. For the **Paint Bucket** tool, the only property you can set is the fill colour. The colour shown here is the colour that will be used next time you use the tool (your colour may be different – this doesn't matter).

▶ Click in the middle of the circle you have drawn with the **Paint Bucket** tool. It should fill with the colour shown in the **Properties** panel.

Figure 2.14: Creating a fill with the Paint Bucket tool

Changing the fill colour

 ▶ Click the **Selection** tool in the **Toolbox**.

▶ Click in the middle of the circle to select the fill. Now change the colour using the **Properties** panel.

Figure 2.15: Selecting a fill

Moving a fill

One quite strange feature of **Flash** is that you can select and move fills and strokes independently.

▶ Select the fill if it is not already selected.

▶ Click and drag the fill to the left away from the outline.

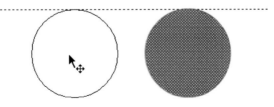

Figure 2.16: Moving a fill away from an outline

Notice that **Flash** gives you a guideline to show when the fill is lined up with the outline.

▶ Drop the fill.

Ink Bottle tool

In the same way that you can add a fill to a stroke, you can also add a stroke to a fill. You do this using the **Ink Bottle** tool.

 ▶ Select the **Ink Bottle** tool from the **Toolbox**. Press the **Escape** key so that the **Properties** panel shows the properties for the **Ink Bottle** tool instead of for the selected shape.

▶ Change the stroke color using the **Properties** panel.

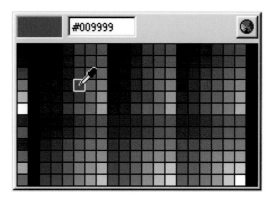

Figure 2.17: The Color Palette

▶ Now click the **Ink Bottle** on the circle fill on the **Stage**.

Figure 2.18: Adding an outline using the Ink Bottle tool

The fill gets an outline (called a **Stroke**).

Overlapping objects

Something strange happens when objects overlap on the **Stage** – we'll look at that now.

 Click the **Selection** tool in the **Toolbox**. Click on the circle without a fill to select it, and drag it so that it overlaps the other one.

> **Tip:** If you accidentally reshape the circle, just select **Edit**, **Undo** from the **Main Menu** bar. Remember to select a shape first before moving it.

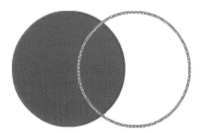

Figure 2.19: Overlapping objects

 Now click and drag a piece of fill. It's been cut by the other line!

Figure 2.20: Overlapping objects

 Break up the image by selecting the strokes of the circles and moving them around.

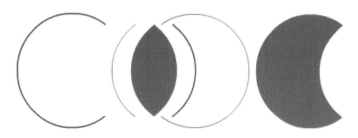

Figure 2.21

 Click and drag a box round part of a shape using the **Selection** tool.

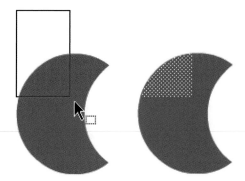

Figure 2.22: Selecting part of a shape using a selection box

▶   Click and drag the selection.

Figure 2.23

When you use a selection box to select shapes, you must be very careful to make sure the selection box contains everything you need; otherwise it will break apart your shapes when you move the selection.

Tip: You can use **Edit**, **Undo** to undo your last action.

Save and Close

O When you've finished, select **File, Close** from the **Main Menu** bar. If you haven't recently saved, you'll be prompted to save the document. Click **Yes** at the prompt.

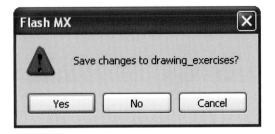

Figure 2.24: Saving changes

Immediately the original **Start Page** pops up again!

Tip: If you'd rather use the **File** menu to create and open documents, tick the small box on the bottom left of the **Start Page**, labelled **Don't Show Again**. If you can't see this box, it is probably hidden behind the **Properties** panel – collapse the panel then try. You'll have to select something from the **Start Page** to make it disappear, but it won't come back.

Figure 2.25: The Start Page reappears

O If this is the end of a session and you want to close **Flash**, select **File, Exit** from the **Main Menu** bar. If not, leave it open for the next chapter.

Editing Objects

3

In the next few chapters we will build up an animated weather map; at the end you will have an animated movie of a five day weather forecast, similar to one you might see on the weather forecast on TV.

The first step is to draw the weather symbols and the background map. We'll then animate the symbols to move across the map.

Let's be optimistic and start with a sunny symbol.

- ◐ Open **Flash** if it is not already open, and select **Create New Flash Document** from the **Start Page**. (Alternatively, select **File**, **New**, **Flash Document** from the **Main Menu** bar.)

 ◐ Select the **Oval** tool in the **Toolbox**.

◐ We don't want to snap to objects, so make sure that the **Snap to Objects** icon, in the **Options** section at the bottom of the **Toolbox**, isn't pressed in.

Setting the tool properties

◉   Change the colours of the stroke and the fill in the **Properties** panel to approximately match those shown below. Make sure the stroke is **Solid** with a width of **3**.

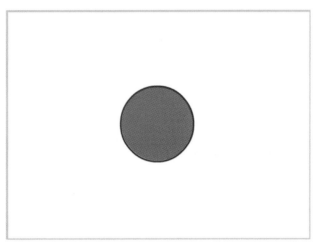

Figure 3.1: The Properties panel showing the Oval tool properties

We are going to draw a circle in the middle of the **Stage**.

◉   Click and drag whilst holding down the **Shift** key, which will constrain the oval to be a perfect circle. Release the mouse when you're happy with the circle.

Figure 3.2: A circle is just a special type of oval

Erasing the stroke

Flash can be quite confusing because there are many different ways to do the same thing.

One way to delete the stroke would be to select it with the **Selection** tool and then press the **Delete** key. Instead, we will use the **Eraser** tool.

The Eraser tool

 Select the **Eraser** tool from the **Toolbox**.

There are a few options to choose from at the bottom of the **Toolbox**.

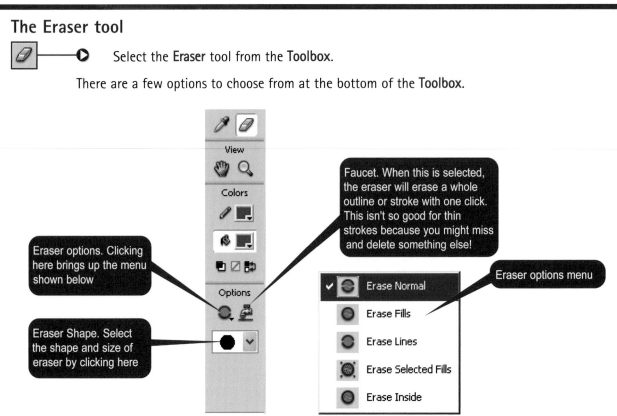

Figure 3.3: Eraser tool options in the Toolbox

Click on the **Eraser options** icon then select **Erase Lines** form the menu that appears.

Tip: Take a look at the other options in the **Eraser options** menu.

 Click and drag the eraser over the outline of the circle. It will look as though you are deleting the fill also, but when you release the mouse button the fill will reappear. Make sure the entire outline is erased.

No Stroke and No Fill options

We could have drawn the circle without a stroke in the first place.

Press the **Escape** key to make sure nothing is selected.

Click the **Oval** tool in the **Toolbox**.

- ● In the **Properties** panel, click the colour box next to the **Stroke** icon.

- ● In the colour palette, click the **No Stroke** icon in the top right.

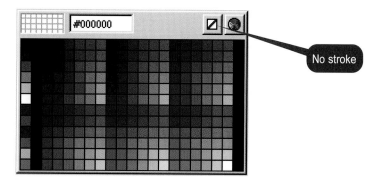

Figure 3.4: The Color Palette

- ● Draw a circle with no stroke to check it works.

Drawing a circle without a fill

 ● With the **Oval** tool still selected, click the colour box in the **Properties** panel next to the **Fill** icon.

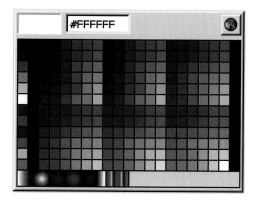

Figure 3.5: The Color Palette

The **No Fill** icon isn't there! This is because you already have the **No Stroke** option selected. **Flash** will not let you draw a shape with no fill and no stroke – quite sensibly!

- ● Use the **Properties** panel to give the stroke a colour.

- ● Now reopen the colour palette for the fill. Select the **No Fill** option.

- ● Draw a circle to check it works.

○ Delete these two extra circles so you're left with the original circle, which should be bright yellow and should have no stroke.

Figure 3.6: Yellow circle as the basis for the sunny symbol

Saving

○ Select **File, Save** from the menu.

○ Create a new folder called **Weather Project**. Save the document as **Symbols** in the new folder. Leave the file type as **Flash MX 2004 Document (*.fla)**.

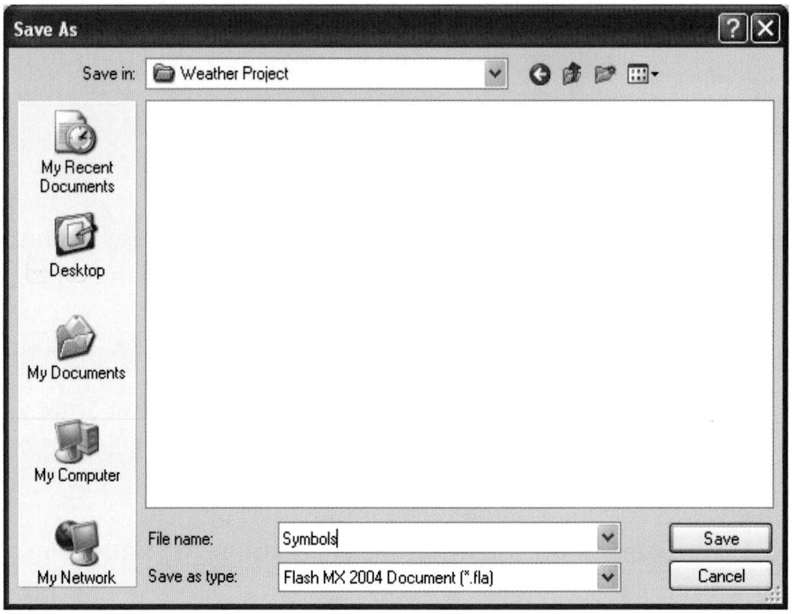

Figure 3.7: The Save As window

The Free Transform tool

The **Free Transform** tool is great for resizing, rotating, skewing and more.

 ▶ Click the **Free Transform** tool in the **Toolbox**.

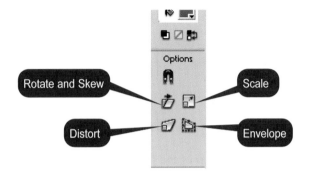

Figure 3.8: Free Transform tool options in the Toolbox

Envelope

 ▶ Click on the yellow circle. Now click the **Envelope** icon at the bottom of the **Toolbox**.

Figure 3.9: The Envelope option of the Free Transform tool

An envelope is created around the circle. The small black squares are called **nodes**.

▶ Click and drag a few of the nodes to reshape the circle.

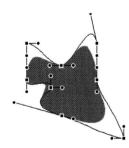

Figure 3.10: The Envelope option of the Free Transform tool

Interesting!

Rotate and Skew

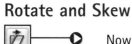 ▶ Now click the **Rotate and Skew** icon at the bottom of the **Toolbox**.

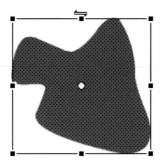

Figure 3.11: The Rotate and Skew option of the Free Transform tool – preparing to skew

▶ To skew the shape, place the mouse pointer over one of the nodes along a side, as shown in Figure 3.11. Click and drag to skew the shape; release the mouse when you're happy with the effect.

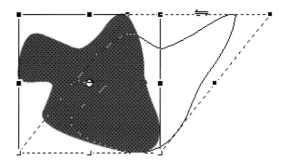

Figure 3.12: The Rotate and Skew option of the Free Transform tool – skew in progress

▶ To rotate a shape, hover the mouse pointer near a corner node.

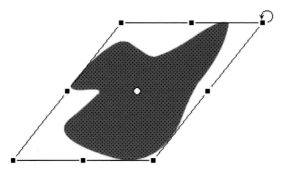

Figure 3.13: The Rotate and Skew option of the Free Transform tool – preparing to rotate

▶ Click and drag to rotate the shape.

Scale

 ◗ Click the **Scale** icon at the bottom of the **Toolbox**.

◗ To resize an object whilst preserving its proportions, click and drag a corner node. To stretch an object, use one of the nodes along the sides. Try both types of scaling.

Revert

When you've been playing about with a drawing, making changes that you don't want to save, the **Revert** command can be very useful. **Revert** simply sets the drawing back to the last saved version.

◗ When you've finished experimenting with the **Free Transform** tool options, select **File, Revert** from the menu to revert to the saved file.

Figure 3.14: Reverting to the last saved version

◗ Click **Revert** at the prompt.

Stage level and Overlay level objects

The circle we are working on is a **Stage level** object. All objects start out as **Stage level** objects. At **Stage level**, outlines can be moved independently of fills, and objects get cut away if they overlap. **Overlay** objects are more stable; this is good once you have drawn an object and don't want the outline and fill getting separated, or half the object disappearing because another object has overlapped it.

There are two ways to turn a **Stage level** object into an **Overlay level** object:

1. **Group** it, either on its own or with another object (this includes grouping an outline with its fill).

2. Turn the object into a **symbol** (we'll cover this in Chapter 4).

Turning the circle into an Overlay level object

We'll do this by grouping the fill. It doesn't matter that we will not be grouping it with anything else.

 ● Select the circle using the **Selection** tool.

● Select **Modify, Group** from the menu.

Figure 3.15: Grouping an object

A solid outline appears around the circle.

● Now draw another circle overlapping this one using the **Oval** tool in the **Toolbox**. Try moving the circle using the **Selection** tool; it doesn't get cut away! The **Stage level** objects don't interact at all with **Overlay level** objects. Notice that **Stage level** objects are always placed behind **Overlay level** objects. Delete the extra circle when you're finished.

● You could reverse this and make the circle a **Stage level** object again by first selecting it, then choosing **Modify, Ungroup** from the menu. Leave it as an **Overlay level** object for now though.

Drawing lines

Before drawing any more, we'll quickly change the background colour of the document.

● Click the **Selection** tool in the **Toolbox**, then press the **Escape** key to deselect everything. In the **Properties** panel, click on the box titled **Background**. Choose a light blue background colour.

Now we need to add some lines around the circle to represent the sunshine rays. First we'll set the tool properties.

● Select the **Line** tool in the **Toolbox**. Make sure nothing is selected on the **Stage**.

In the **Properties** panel, change the colour to match the yellow of the circle. To do this, click the colour square in the **Properties** panel then click on the yellow sun with the dropper icon. Notice that you are not limited to the colour palette – you can click anywhere on the screen with the dropper to find a colour!

Figure 3.16

Enter **10** as the line width, and leave the line style as **Solid**.

Figure 3.17: The Properties panel showing Line tool properties

Hold down the **Shift** key then click and drag to draw a vertical line through the yellow circle.

Tip: Holding down **Shift** makes it easier to draw a completely vertical line.

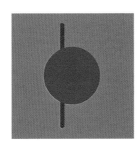

Figure 3.18

We need to reposition the line to be in the centre of the circle.

○   Select the line with the **Selection** tool. The line won't be cut away by the circle because the circle is an **Overlay level** object.

○   Use the arrow keys on the keyboard to finely position the line at the centre of the circle.

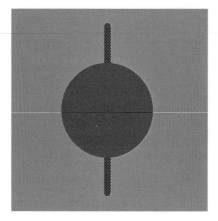

Figure 3.19: First two rays of the sun

The Transform panel

Now for something clever... we'll use the **Transform** panel to copy and rotate this line to give us all the other rays!

○   You probably won't have the **Transform** panel open already. Select **Window, Design Panels, Transform** from the **Main Menu** bar.

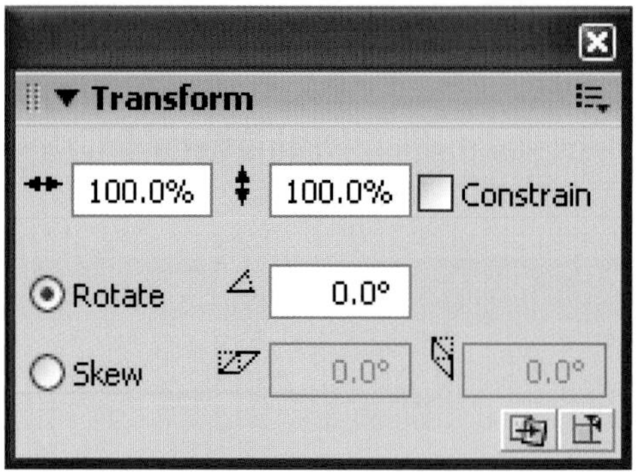

Figure 3.20: The Transform panel

The **Transform** panel opens.

Docking a panel

The Transform panel will most likely have opened in its own window, as shown in Figure 3.20. You can dock it like the other panels down the right-hand side of the screen if you wish:

◉ To dock the panel, click and drag the small dimples at the top left of the panel. Drag the panel over to the right of the screen – you'll see a ghost of the panel to show where it will be placed – and drop it when you're happy with its position.

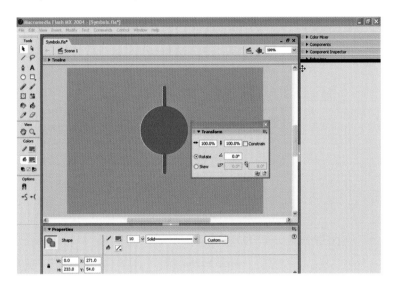

Figure 3.21: Docking a panel

Tip: You can click and drag the panel back onto the **Stage** to undock it again.

Rotating using the Transform panel

◉ With the line selected, copy the settings from Figure 3.22 into the Transform panel.

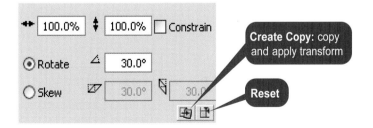

Figure 3.22: Copying and rotating an object using the Transform panel

Notice the two icons in the bottom right of the Transform panel. The one on the left will copy the object then resize, rotate, or skew the copy. The one on the right resets the fields to their default values.

◉ Click the Create Copy icon to copy and rotate the line.

Figure 3.23: Copying and rotating an object using the Transform panel – first copy

 Keep clicking the **Create Copy** icon until all the sun's rays are drawn.

Figure 3.24: Copying and rotating an object using the Transform panel – fifth copy

Looks good! Now we are going to create a small gap between the rays and the yellow circle. To do this, we will take advantage of the cut-away feature.

Turning an Overlay object into a Stage level object

In order to use the cut-away feature, we'll have to turn the sun back into a **Stage level** object by ungrouping it.

 With the **Selection** tool, click the yellow circle.

 Select **Modify, Ungroup** from the menu.

Figure 3.25: Turning an Overlay level object into a Stage level object

If we moved the circle now, it would not cut away the rays. We have to deselect it first, then reselect it.

◉   Click away from the circle to deselect it.

◉   Now reselect the circle by clicking it.

     ◉   Click the **Free Transform** tool in the **Toolbox**.

◉   Hold down the both the **Shift** and **Alt** keys, then click and drag a corner of the transform box to shrink the sun.

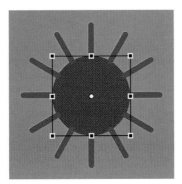 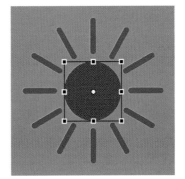

Figure 3.26

Tip: Holding down the **Shift** key keeps the proportions of the circle. Holding down the **Alt** key resizes the circle about its centre.

◉   Clear the selection by pressing the **Escape** key or just clicking away from the circle.

Save

◉   Save the sun by selecting **File**, **Save** from the **Main Menu** bar, or by using the shortcut keys **Ctrl-S**.

◉   Close the image either by clicking the small **x** icon at the top right of the **Stage** or by selecting **File**, **Close** from the menu.

Figure 3.27: Closing a file using the x icon

Symbols and the Library

4

In this chapter we'll make the sun graphic into a **symbol**. Symbols are stored in the **Library**. By making the sun a **symbol**, we can reuse the graphic over and over again, simply by pulling it from the **Library** onto the **Stage**. This is something we'll use later when we start creating the weather map and we need many instances of each symbol.

Opening a recent file

◉ From the opening screen, the **Symbols.fla** file should be visible. Click it if you can see it; if you can't, select **File**, **Open** from the **Main Menu** bar, then find the **Symbols.fla** file in the **Weather Project** folder.

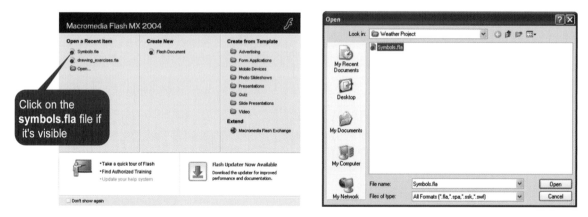

Figure 4.1: Opening a recent file

Tip: You could also select **File**, **Open Recent** from the **Main Menu** bar. Click the file you want from the menu that appears, if it is listed.

Grouping the sun picture

We need to group the sun for two reasons: we want the circle to stay where it is relative to the rays, and a picture must be made an **Overlay level** object before it can be made into a symbol. Remember that one way to make something an **Overlay level** object is to group it.

 With the **Selection** tool, draw a large selection box around the whole sun picture to select it.

Figure 4.2

Tip: Another way to select the entire image is to select **Edit, Select All** from the **Main Menu** bar.

 Select **Modify, Group** from the menu.

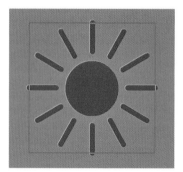

Figure 4.3

 Try moving the sun around using the **Selection** tool. The rays are now firmly attached to the sun.

Resizing the Sun

We'll resize the sun symbol to be about 1 to 1.5 cm wide. Yours is probably quite a bit bigger than this at the moment.

 Select **View, Rulers** from the **Main Menu** bar. The rulers appear around the **Work Area**.

Changing ruler units

We'll change the ruler units to **centimetres**.

 Deselect everything by pressing the **Escape** key. In the **Properties** panel, click the button next to where it says **Size**.

Figure 4.4: The Properties panel showing the document properties

 At the bottom of the window, change the **Ruler units** to **Centimeters**. Click **OK**.

Figure 4.5: The Document Properties window

 Click the **Free Transform** tool in the **Toolbox**. Click the sun.

 Hold down the **Shift** key then click and drag a corner of the transform box to make the sun smaller. Use the rulers to size the sun to be between **1 cm** and **1.5 cm**. Use the **Zoom** tool if necessary.

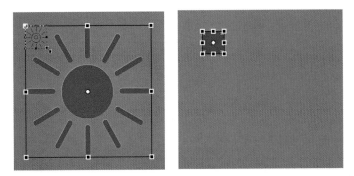

Figure 4.6: Shrinking the sun

Editing Grouped Objects

At this size, the width of the rays is far too thick. We'll edit the rays and change the line width to **3**. We don't need to ungroup the object for this; there is a way of editing grouped objects.

◉   First take a look at the top of the **Stage**. It just says **Scene 1** at the moment.

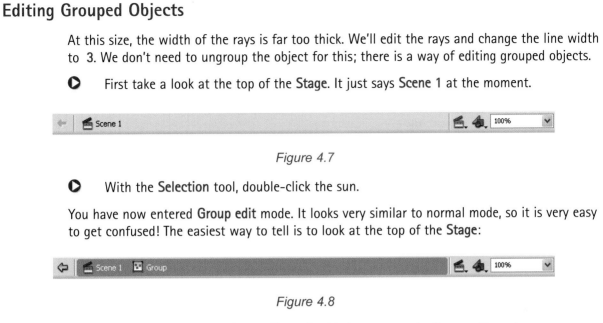

Figure 4.7

◉   With the **Selection** tool, double-click the sun.

You have now entered **Group edit** mode. It looks very similar to normal mode, so it is very easy to get confused! The easiest way to tell is to look at the top of the **Stage**:

Figure 4.8

This has changed. Whenever it says **Group** in this bar, you are in **Group edit** mode.

Editing the sun

We need to select all the rays but not the central circle.

◉   First zoom in using the **Zoom** tool.

◉   Choose **Edit**, **Select All** on the **Main Menu** bar. This selects all the shapes.

◉   Now hold down the **Shift** key, then click the central yellow circle to deselect it.

Figure 4.9

◉   In the **Properties** panel, change the line width to **3** by typing it into the line width box, then pressing **Enter**. The slider can be pretty awkward, so I would advise typing in the line width.

◉   Deselect by clicking away from the sun.

Exiting Group edit mode

To exit **Group edit** mode, either:

◉   Double-click away from the object you're editing, *or*

◉   Click once where it says **Scene 1** at the top of the **Stage**.

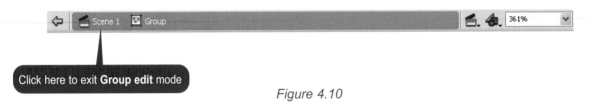

Figure 4.10

The blue selection box reappears around the object.

Figure 4.11

The Library panel

◉   First make sure you can see the **Library** panel. If not, select **Window**, **Library** from the Main Menu bar.

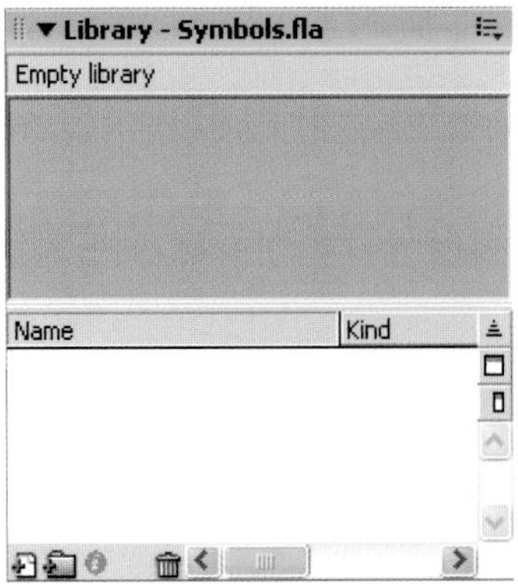

Figure 4.12: The Library panel

As you can see, the **Library** is currently empty. We will turn the sun picture into a symbol that will be added to the **Library**. When you have finished creating all the other weather symbols, the **Library** will be full of symbols that you can use in your animations.

Creating a Symbol

○ Make sure the sun is selected – click it with the Selection tool if it isn't.

○ Select Modify, Convert to Symbol from the Main Menu bar. Type Sun as the Name, set the Behavior to Graphic, and select the central Registration point (used for rotation and alignment).

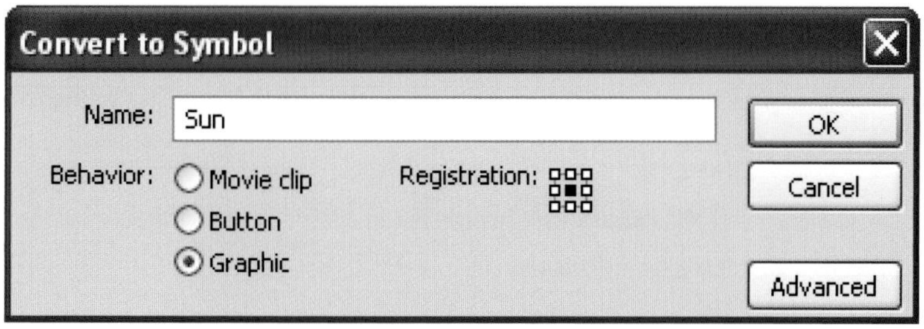

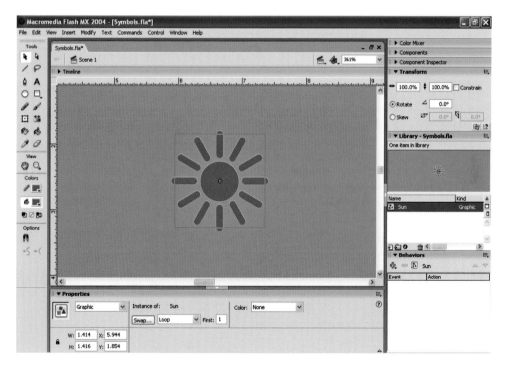

Figure 4.13: The Create New Symbol window

○ Click OK. Now look in the Library panel: the Sun symbol is listed.

Figure 4.14: The new Sun symbol is added to the Library

○ Save the document by pressing Ctrl-S.

Symbol instances

When you have many copies of a symbol, each copy is called an **instance**. It actually doesn't use up much more memory having 100 instances of a symbol than having just one. This is because Flash only needs to know each instance's position, and maybe if there are any other deviations from the original symbol; it doesn't actually copy the symbol.

We'll have a go at creating many instances of the sun symbol on the **Stage**.

▶ With the **Selection** tool, click and drag the **Sun** symbol from the **Library** panel onto the **Stage**. Try clicking and dragging from the two different places marked in the screenshot below.

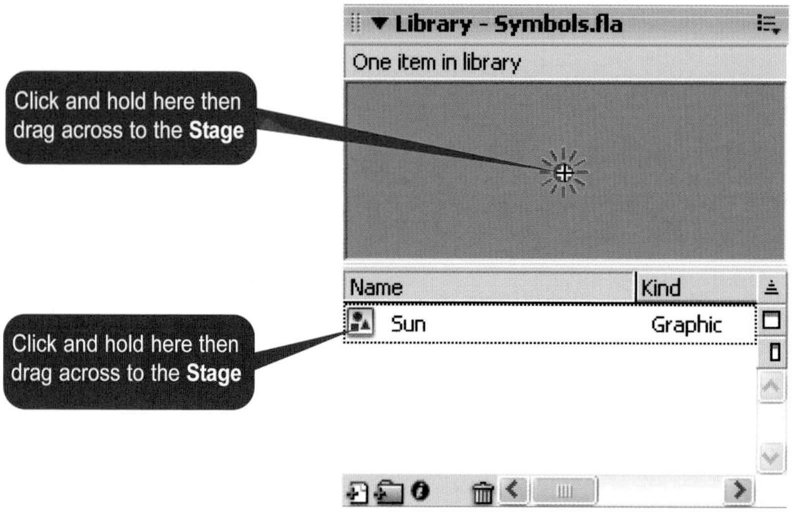

Figure 4.15: The Library panel

▶ Try moving the suns around on the **Stage**; you can move an instance in just the same way as you can the original.

Figure 4.16

Editing a symbol

You can edit symbols in **Symbol edit** mode. This is very similar to **Group edit** mode, which you have already used.

 First have a look at the top of the **Stage**.

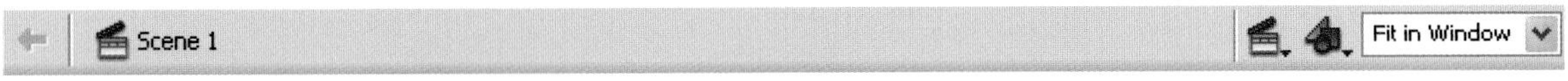

Figure 4.17

 Double-click one of the sun instances on the **Stage** with the **Selection** tool. Take a look at the top of the **Stage** now.

Figure 4.18

The word **Sun** has appeared, to show that you are in **Symbol edit** mode working with the symbol called **Sun**.

> **Tip:** If you don't like double-clicking, you can right-click the symbol and select **Edit** from the menu that appears.

Because the symbol is grouped, we can't actually edit it without delving into another layer of detail – we'll do this now.

 Double-click the same sun again.

Figure 4.19

The bar at the top of the **Stage** shows that you are now in **Group edit** mode, within **Symbol edit** mode.

◉   Click the centre circle of the sun. In the **Properties** panel, select a **red** colour.

Figure 4.20

All the instances change! This is a particularly useful feature of symbols and instances – to make a change you only need to edit the symbol, not every instance.

◉   Press **Ctrl-Z** on the keyboard to undo the change.

Exiting Symbol edit mode

◉   First, return to **Symbol edit** mode from **Group edit** mode by clicking where it says **Sun** at the top of the **Stage**.

◉   Now click where it says **Scene 1** to return to normal editing mode.

> **Tip:** You could have just clicked **Scene 1** to exit both **Group edit** mode and **Symbol edit** mode with one click.

Editing an instance not a symbol

What if you want to change an instance without all other instances of the same symbol changing? We'll try this now.

These effects are best demonstrated on a coloured background, so we'll change the colour of the **Stage**.

◉ Click on a blank part of the **Stage** to deselect everything.

◉ In the **Properties** panel, change the background colour to a dark green.

▼ **Properties**						
Document	Size:	19.3 x 14.04 cm	Background: ■	Frame rate: 12	fps	
Symbols.fla	Publish:	Settings...	Player: 7	ActionScript: 2	Profile: Default	

Figure 4.21: The Properties panel for the Symbols file

◉ Click once on one of the suns on the **Stage**.

◉ Make sure you're not in **Symbol edit** or **Group edit** mode – to do this look at the top of the **Stage**, which should look like the one below. If yours has additional entries for **Sun** or **Group**, just click once where it says **Scene 1**.

Yours should just say **Scene 1**, as shown here

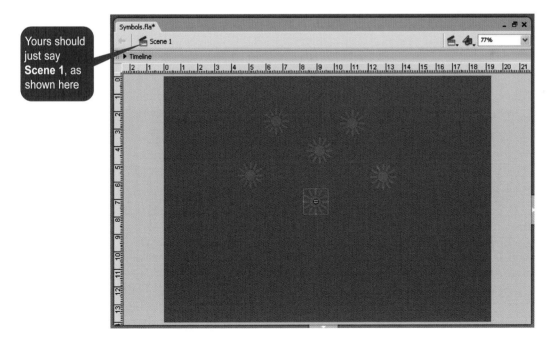

Figure 4.22

○ Now look at the **Properties** panel:

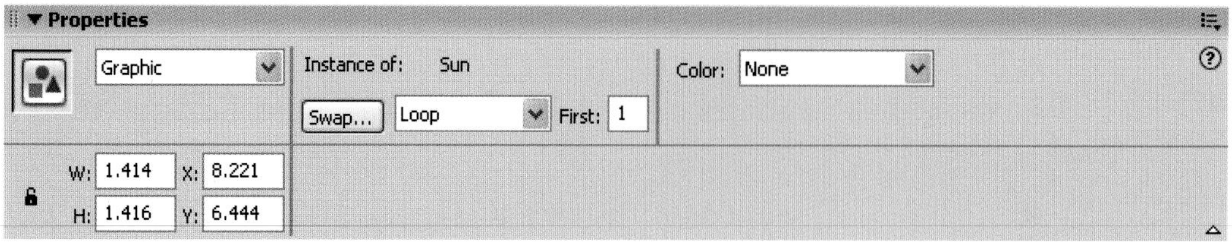

Figure 4.23: The Properties panel showing the properties of a symbol instance

There are a few options here for changing the appearance of an instance. We'll look at all the options on the **Color** menu.

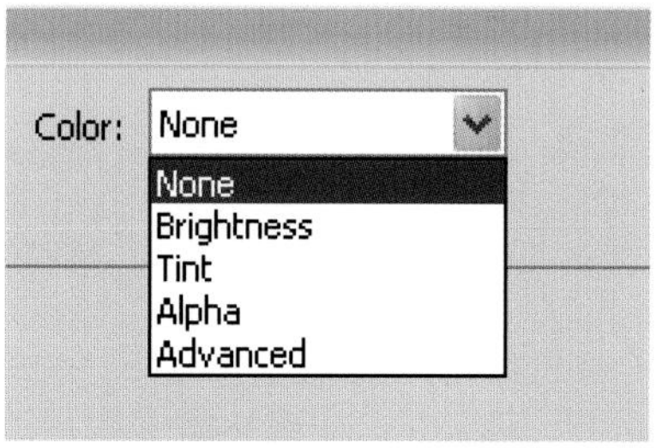

Figure 4.24: Changing the properties of a symbol instance

Brightness

○ Select **Brightness** from the **Color** list in the **Properties** panel.

○ Type **50** into the **Brightness** box then press **Enter**.

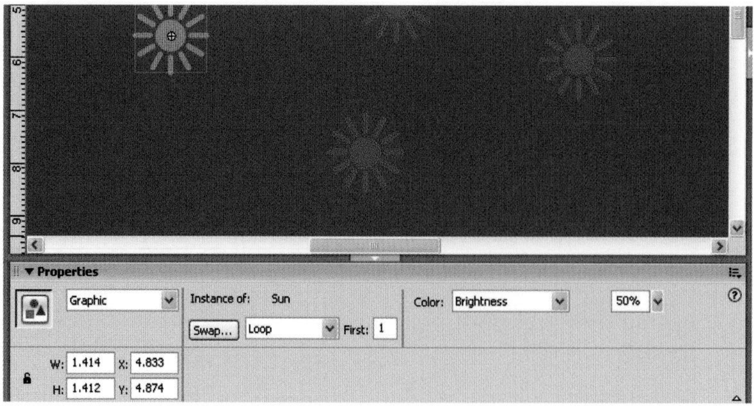

Figure 4.25: Changing the brightness of an instance

The selected sun is brighter – it looks like it's faded. Notice that only the selected sun has changed; the symbol itself has not been altered.

Tint

 Click a different sun with the **Selection** tool.

 Select **Tint** from the **Color** list in the **Properties**.

Tint basically adds a layer of colour on top of the original symbol. The box with the percentage (which probably says 50%) controls the opacity of the tint layer – the lower the percentage, the more the original colour shows through. We'll change this to 100% so that you cannot see through the tint layer.

 First, click the small colour box in the **Properties** panel. Pick a different colour from the palette.

 Now change the opacity of the tint layer. Type **100** into the opacity field then press **Enter**. Your **Properties** panel should look like the one below.

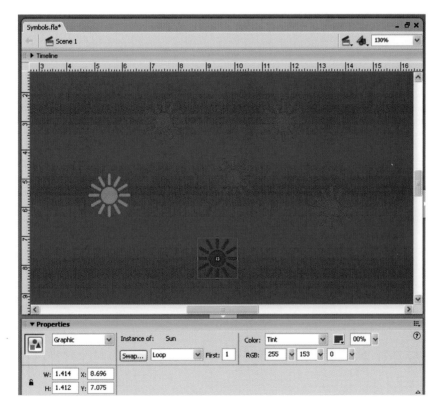

Figure 4.26: Changing the colour of an instance

Alpha

Alpha sets the transparency of an object. It is the most processor-intensive effect available, so use it sparingly! For symbols on a white background you should use **Brightness** instead of **Alpha** because it will give the same effect but will use much less processor power.

 Select another, unaltered, sun.

 In the **Properties** panel select **Alpha** from the **Color** list.

- Type **50** into the **Properties** panel then press **Enter**.

The sun becomes partially transparent so you can see the green background through the yellow sun.

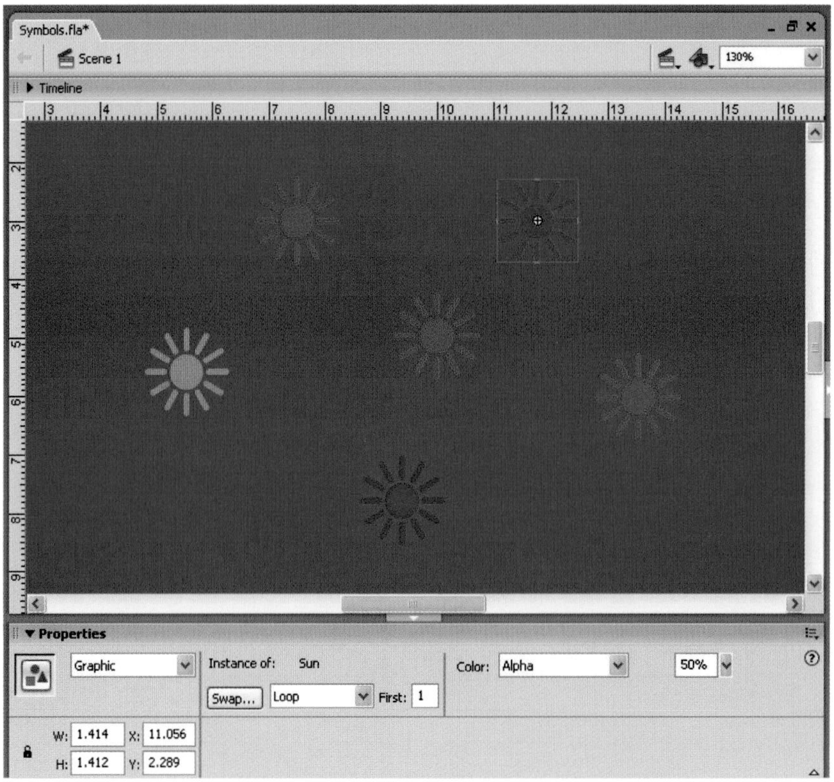

![Figure 4.27: Screenshot of Symbols.fla showing several sun graphics on a dark background with the Properties panel below showing a Graphic instance of Sun with Color set to Alpha at 50%]

Figure 4.27: Changing the transparency of an instance

- Save your file.

Publishing

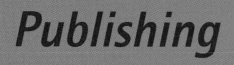

This chapter describes how to view the symbols document in an Internet browser. At the moment, this picture can only be viewed by people with the **Flash** authoring software. We will save it in a format that anyone with an Internet browser can view.

You can skip this chapter for now if you like, and refer back to it when you need to publish your project.

When you save a **Flash** file in a format that can be viewed outside the **Flash** authoring environment, this is called **publishing**. You can publish pictures and movies in much the same way.

◉ Load up **Flash** and open the **Symbols.fla** file.

◉ Select **File, Publish Settings** from the **Main Menu** bar.

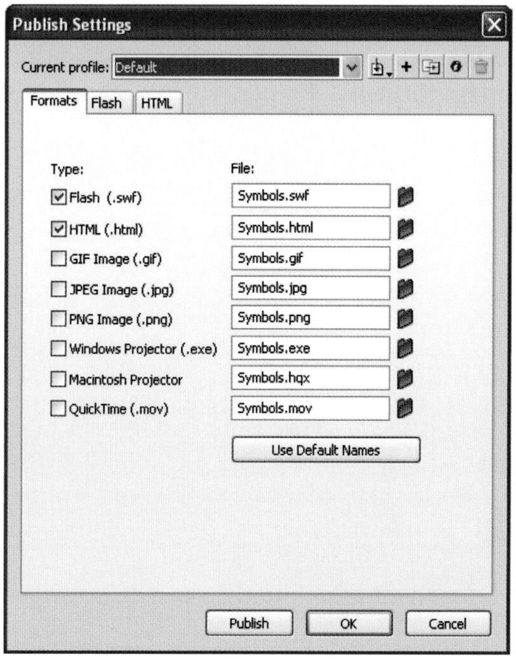

Figure 5.1: The Publish Settings window

There are a lot of file types to choose from here!

 Make sure the **HTML** and **Flash** checkboxes are ticked as shown in Figure 5.1. When you tick **HTML, Flash** is automatically ticked too.

These settings mean that two files will be created when you click **Publish** – an **HTML (.html)** file and a **Flash Shockwave (.swf)** file.

Choosing file names and locations

You can give the files different names and specify where they will be saved.

 Click the folder icon to the right of the top box for the **Flash** file.

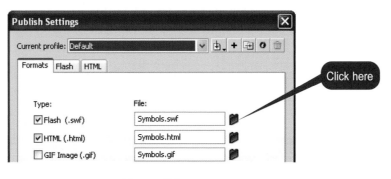

Figure 5.2

 Make sure the file is stored in the **Weather Project** folder. Leave the name as **Symbols**.

Figure 5.3: Choosing a location for the published files

○   Click **Save**. Repeat this for the **HTML** file.

○   Click the **Flash** tab at the top of the **Publish Settings** window. Copy the settings from Figure 5.4(a). Now click the **HTML** tab and copy the settings from Figure 5.4(b).

> **Tip:** A tab is created in the **Publish Settings** window for each of the file formats you tick on the first page, with the exception of **Projector** files.

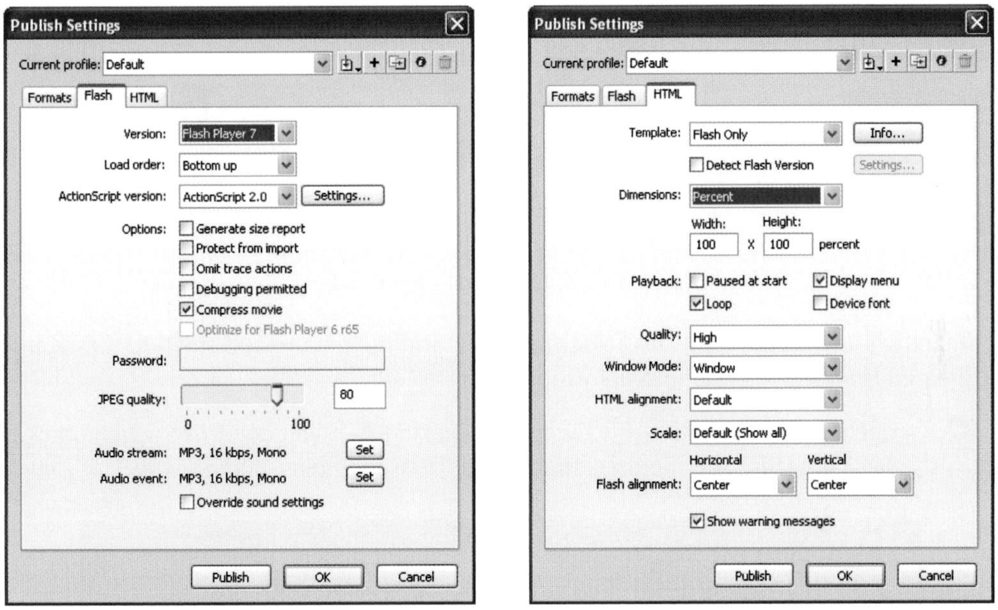

Figure 5.4: The Publish Settings window for (a) Flash, (b) HTML

> **Tip:** If you want your image to appear on a transparent background, select **Transparent Windowless** from the **Window Mode** option under the **HTML** tab in the Publish Settings window.

○   Click Publish.

A window will pop up to tell you that it is publishing.

○   Click **OK** to close the **Publish Settings** window.

Viewing the symbols file in a browser

○   Open up **Windows Explorer**, or whichever program you use to view the files on your computer.

> **Tip:** To open **Windows Explorer**, right-click the **Start** menu at the bottom left of the screen then select **Explore** from the menu that appears.

○   Locate the **Weather Project** folder and open it.

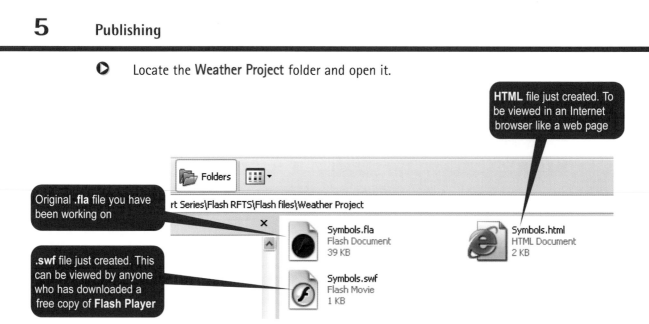

Figure 5.5: Opening a published file from Windows Explorer

There will be three files in this folder now: the original picture and the two files you have just created from the **Publish Settings** window.

○   Open the **Symbols.html** file by double-clicking it. If you don't like double-clicking, you can right-click the file then select **Open** from the menu that appears.

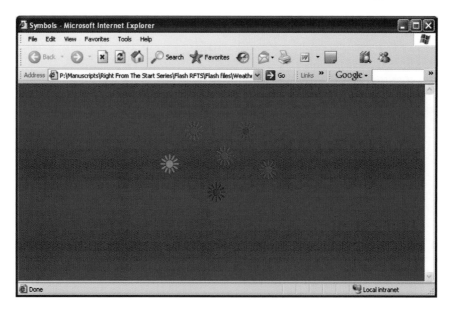

Figure 5.6: Viewing the published HTML file in Internet Explorer

○   Try resizing the browser window. Notice that the picture resizes to fit. This is because we selected the **Dimensions** in the **Publish** window to be **100 percent**. If we had specified a size in pixels, the picture wouldn't resize.

○   Close the browser window.

Publish Preview

You can preview what the published Flash (.swf) file will look like. This is useful because is very quick and easy; Flash regenerates the published document and opens it.

○ Select File, Publish Preview, Flash from the Main Menu bar. The document is shown on a separate sheet in Flash.

Figure 5.7: Publish Preview

○ To return to editing the movie, just click the Symbols.fla sheet tab at the top of the page. You can either leave the other sheet open, or right-click its tab and then select Close from the menu that appears.

Tip: We will use this preview a lot throughout the book. There is a shortcut you can use instead of using the **File** menu – just press **Ctrl-Enter**.

○ Save the Symbols.fla document by pressing Ctrl-S on the keyboard, then close it.

Symbol Edit Mode 6

We've already created the **Sun** symbol and added it to the **Library**. There are lots more weather symbols we need to create to make the weather map. In this chapter we'll go through how to create a cloud symbol, then you'll be left on your own to create a few more!

In the last chapter, you drew a sun and then converted it to a symbol. The cloud symbol will be created entirely in **Symbol edit** mode.

○ Open the **Symbols.fla** file either by clicking it on the **Start page** or by selecting **File**, **Open** from the **Main Menu** bar.

Creating a symbol

○ If you can't see the **Library** panel, select **Window**, **Library** from the **Main Menu** bar.

 ○ At the bottom left of the **Library** panel, click the **Add New Symbol** icon.

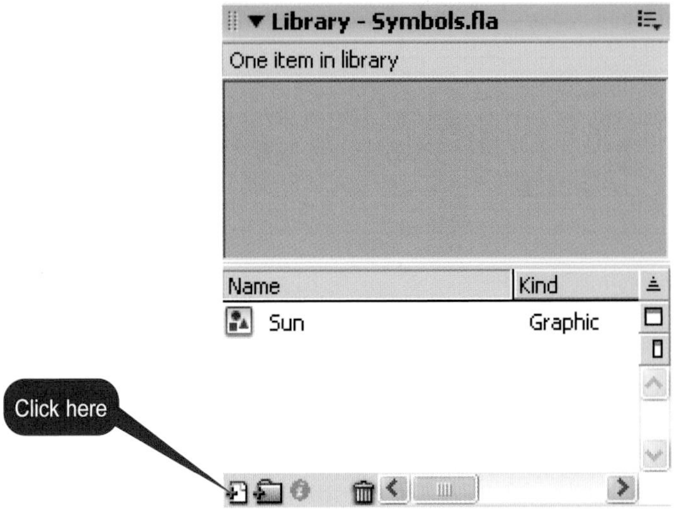

Figure 6.1: The Library panel

○ The **Create New Symbol** window appears. Enter **White Cloud** as the symbol name. Leave the **Behaviour** as **Graphic**.

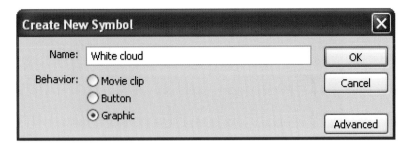

Figure 6.2: Creating a new symbol

○ Click **OK**.

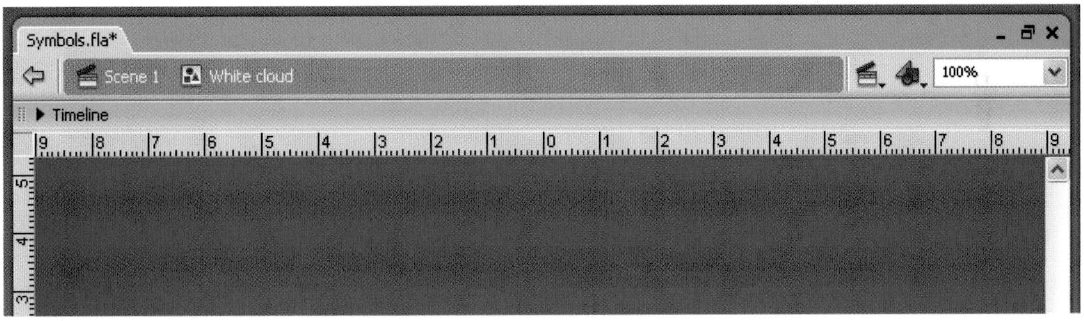

Figure 6.3: Symbol edit mode

You're now in **Symbol edit** mode. You can tell this because it says **White cloud** above the **Stage** next to **Scene 1**.

○ Notice the small target in the middle of the **Stage**. This is the **insertion point** for the symbol. We need to draw the cloud on top of this target.

○ Select the **Zoom** tool from the **Toolbox**. Make sure the **Zoom in** option is selected at the bottom of the **Toolbox** then click once on the target in the middle of the **Stage**.

○ Select the **Line** tool from the **Toolbox**.

○ Make sure nothing is selected, then copy the settings from the screenshot below to the **Properties** panel.

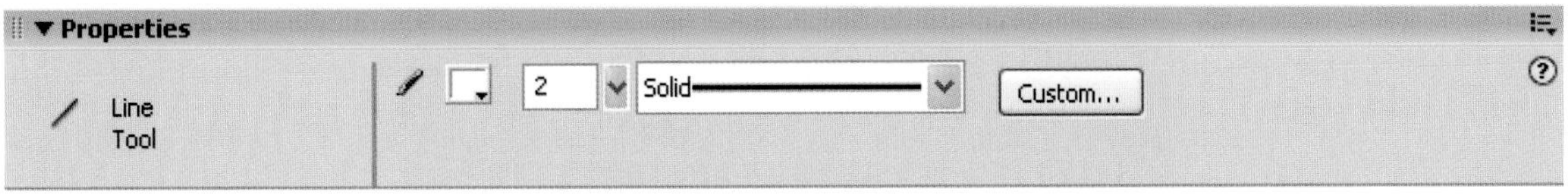

Figure 6.4: The Properties panel showing the Line tool properties

○ Holding down the **Shift** key, click and drag a horizontal line near the target as shown below.

Figure 6.5

○ If you're not happy with the position, use the **Selection** tool to first select the line, then click and drag or use the arrow keys to reposition it.

 ○ Now click the **Oval** tool from the **Toolbox**. Set the line colour to **white**, thickness to **2** and **no fill**.

○ Click and drag out an oval away from the line. Use the **Selection** tool to reposition the oval as shown below. Remember you must select a shape before clicking and dragging it, otherwise you'll reshape it.

> **Tip:** If you make a mistake, just select **Edit**, **Undo** from the **Main Menu** bar. Alternatively, you can press **Ctrl-Z**.

 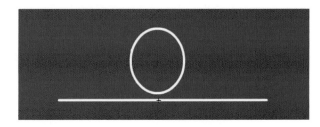

Figure 6.6

○ Draw a circle away from the existing shapes, then use the **Selection** tool to select and drag the circle as shown in Figure 6.7.

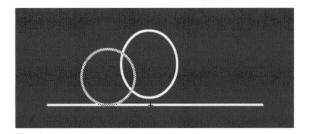

Figure 6.7

Tip: If you find that the circle keeps trying to snap to things, turn off the **Snap** option by clicking the magnet icon at the bottom of the **Toolbox**.

- ◉ While the second circle is selected, go to **Edit, Copy** on the **Main Menu** bar. Now select **Edit, Paste in Center** from the **Main Menu** bar.

- ◉ The circle has been copied; click and drag the circle with the **Selection** tool as shown below.

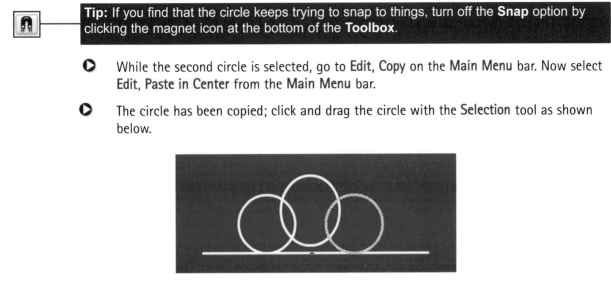

Figure 6.8

Deleting lines

Now we'll use the cut-away feature of **Flash** to neatly cut away all the bits of lines we don't want.

- ◉ First deselect everything. Then, with the **Selection** tool, click to select one of the lines on the inside of the cloud shape (see the screenshot below). Press the **Delete** key.

Figure 6.9

The line disappears!

▶ Delete the other lines so that you are left with a cloud outline. If you need a larger view, click the **Zoom** tool in the **Toolbox** and draw a box around the area you want to zoom in on. Look back at Chapter 1 for more on the **Zoom** options.

Figure 6.10

▶ Click the left-hand circle with the **Selection** tool. Use the arrow keys to nudge it to the right. Delete all the extra bits of line except one, as shown below.

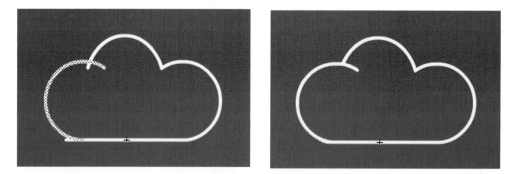

Figure 6.11

▶ Try this again on the other side; this time delete a bit of the right-hand circle rather than the middle circle.

Figure 6.12

Don't worry about the size of the cloud, we'll resize it later.

Grouping the cloud

Grouping the cloud will turn it into an **Overlay level** object.

 With the **Selection** tool, select the whole cloud. Now select **Modify**, **Group** from the menu.

 With the **Selection** tool, position the cloud over the central target.

Figure 6.13: Grouping the symbol

We don't need to turn it into a symbol because it already is one – we have created the cloud entirely in **Symbol edit** mode.

We will need to resize the cloud, but don't do it yet.

Exiting Symbol edit mode

 At the top of the **Stage**, click where it says **Scene 1**.

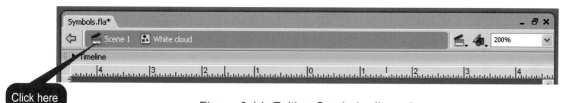

Figure 6.14: Exiting Symbol edit mode

You are returned to the **Symbols.fla** document.

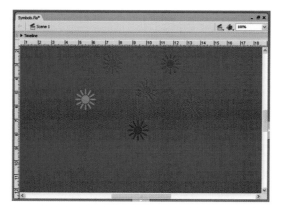

Figure 6.15

Reopening Symbol edit mode

▶ Double-click the icon next to where it says White cloud in the Library panel.

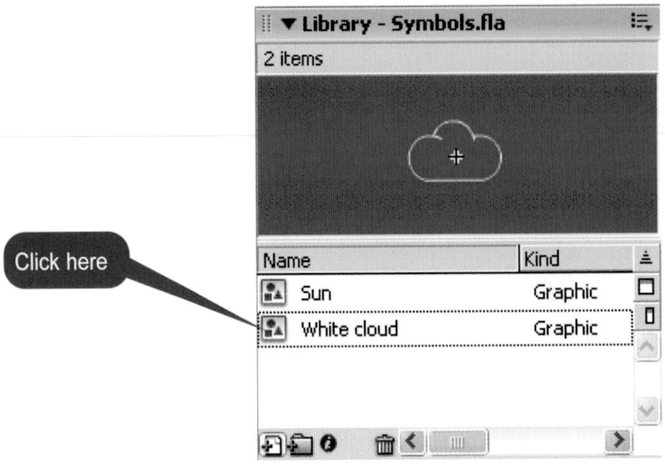

Figure 6.16: The Library panel

In the last chapter we edited the symbols in their place, by double-clicking an instance on the Stage. By double-clicking in the Library panel you are editing the symbol on a Stage of its own. Both views achieve the same effect – it just depends on whether you want to see the changes of the symbol against other objects on the Stage.

▶ Close Symbol edit mode by clicking where it says Scene 1 above the Stage.

▶ Click and drag some instances of the White cloud symbol from the Library panel onto the Stage. You might find they look a bit big next to the suns!

Figure 6.17

We'll resize them now.

○ Double-click one of the clouds on the **Stage**.

You have just entered **Symbol edit** mode, but because you double-clicked an instance on the **Stage**, rather than the symbol in the **Library**, you can edit the symbol in place. This is useful here because we can size the cloud relative to the sun symbols.

○ Select the **Free Transform** tool in the **Toolbox**. Resize the cloud to match the size of the **Sun** symbol; remember to hold down the **Shift** key so that the cloud retains its proportions. Notice that all the other **White cloud** instances change also.

○ Exit **Symbol edit** mode by clicking **Scene 1** above the **Stage**.

> **Tip:** You might want to re-enter **Symbol edit** mode by double-clicking the **White cloud** symbol in the **Library** just to reposition the cloud over the insertion point.

Creating the Black cloud symbol

We'll create a **Black cloud** symbol by turning one instance of the **White cloud** symbol black, then resaving it as a separate symbol.

○ With the **Selection** tool, click one of the **White cloud** instances on the **Stage**.

○ In the **Properties** panel, select **Tint** from the **Color** list, then pick black from the colour palette. Make sure the opacity is **100%**.

Figure 6.18: Changing the tint of a symbol instance

○ Keep the black cloud selected, and choose **Modify**, **Convert to Symbol** from the **Main Menu** bar.

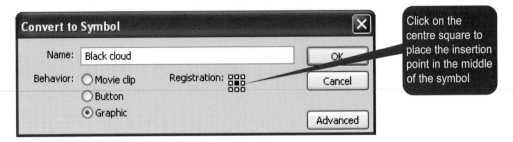

Figure 6.19: Creating a new symbol

○ Name the symbol **Black cloud** then click **OK**. The **Black cloud** symbol is added to the **Library** panel.

○ Drag some more **Black cloud** instances from the **Library** panel onto the **Stage**.

Figure 6.20

○ Double-click a **White cloud** symbol on the **Stage** to enter **Symbol** edit mode. Resize the symbol using the **Free Transform** tool. Notice that the **Black cloud** symbol changes too! Press **Ctrl-Z** to undo the resize.

Despite being its own symbol, the **Black cloud** symbol is still based on the **White cloud** symbol. If you change the size or shape of the **White cloud** symbol, the **Black cloud** symbol will change too. The reverse is not true – you can resize the **Black cloud** symbol without affecting the **White cloud** symbol.

Creating a rain cloud

The **Black cloud** symbol will be the basis of the **Rain cloud** symbol.

◐   Exit **Symbol edit** mode by clicking **Scene 1** above the **Stage**.

◐   With the **Selection** tool, click an instance of the **Black cloud** symbol on the **Stage**.

◐   Select **Modify, Convert to Symbol** from the **Main Menu** bar.

Convert to Symbol	☒
Name: `Rain cloud`	OK
Behavior: ○ Movie clip Registration: ▦	Cancel
○ Button	
⦿ Graphic	Advanced

Figure 6.21: The Convert to Symbol window

◐   Name the symbol **Rain cloud**. Leave the **Behaviour** as **Graphic** for now – we'll change it to **Movie clip** later. Click **OK**.

◐   Double-click the **Rain cloud** symbol in the **Library** panel (not on the **Stage**). Check that it says **Rain cloud** above the **Stage** to show you're in **Symbol edit** mode.

🔍──◐   Use the **Zoom** tool to draw a box around the cloud to enlarge it.

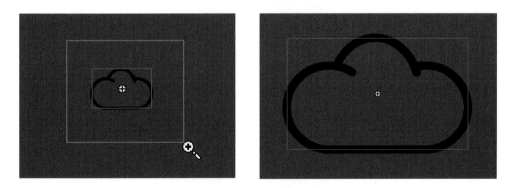

Figure 6.22: Zooming in on the Black cloud symbol

◯──◐   Select the **Oval** tool from the toolbox. In the **Properties** panel, set the **Fill** colour to be blue.

◐   Now click the colour box next to the pencil symbol, then click the **No Stroke** icon.

▶   Draw a small circle away from the cloud.

Figure 6.23

 ▶   Select the **Line** tool from the **Toolbox**. Set the style to **Hairline** in the **Properties** panel. Set the line colour to match the circle you've just drawn. Zoom in on the blue circle then reselect the **Line** tool.

 ▶   At the bottom of the **Toolbox**, click the magnet icon to turn on object snapping.

▶   Draw two lines as shown in the screenshot below; the lines should snap to the sides of the circle. Use the **Selection** tool to reposition the lines if you need to.

Figure 6.24

 ▶   Click the **Paint Bucket** tool in the **Toolbox**. Set the fill colour to match the rest of the rain drop then click in the green triangle to fill in the drop.

Figure 6.25

The Color Mixer panel

We'll apply a radial fill to the raindrop to make it look more rounded.

- Select the raindrop by clicking it with the **Selection** tool.

- If you can't already see the **Color Mixer** panel, select **Window**, **Design Panels**, **Color Mixer** from the **Main Menu** bar.

- In the **Color Mixer** panel, select **Radial** from the list.

Figure 6.26: Choosing a fill type

Now we'll select the colours that will be part of the radial fill. We want to start with a light blue in the middle of the raindrop, changing to dark blue at the edge.

- Follow the steps in the screenshot below to select the light blue colour.

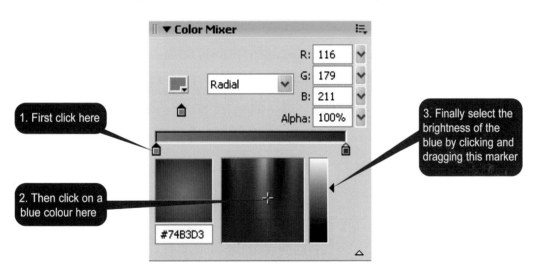

Figure 6.27: The Color Mixer panel

- Now we need to select the dark blue colour. Click on the right-hand colour marker in the **Color Mixer** panel. Follow steps 2 and 3 above to choose a dark blue colour.

● Experiment with clicking and dragging the colour markers, as shown below.

Figure 6.28: The Color Slider in the Color Mixer panel

The Fill Transform tool

We'll use the **Fill Transform** tool to move the central light blue part of the fill down a bit.

 ● Click the **Fill Transform** tool in the **Toolbox**.

● Click on the centre of the raindrop.

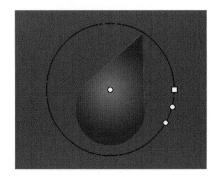

Figure 6.29: Using the Fill Transform tool

By moving the lines and nodes that have appeared, we can alter the fill.

● Click and drag the central node (small white circle) down to look like the screenshot below.

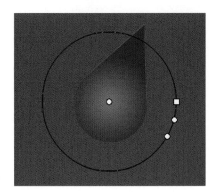

Figure 6.30: Using the Fill Transform tool

● Click away from the raindrop to deselect it. With the **Selection** tool, click to select the two hairline width lines you drew. Change the colour using the **Properties** panel to better match the fill colour.

Figure 6.31

With the **Selection** tool, select the whole raindrop. Now select **Modify, Group** from the menu.

Zoom out using the **Zoom** tool so that you can see both the cloud and the raindrop.

Move the raindrop closer to the cloud and resize it if you need to using the **Free Transform** tool. Move both the cloud and the raindrop so that the insertion point is in the middle of the cloud.

Figure 6.32

Converting the raindrop to a symbol

You may want to use this raindrop in other symbols, so we'll save it in the **Library** by making it a symbol.

Select the raindrop. Go to **Modify, Convert to Symbol** on the **Main Menu** bar.

Figure 6.33

Name the symbol **Raindrop** then click **OK**.

With the **Selection** tool, drag out a second instance of the **Raindrop** from the **Library** to the **Stage** and place it near the first **Raindrop,** slightly overlapping the cloud.

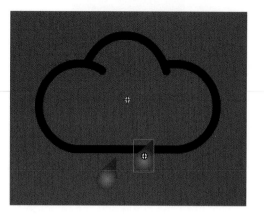

Figure 6.34

 Press **Ctrl-S** to save the **Symbols.fla** file.

Preview the SWF file in Flash

 Select **File, Publish Settings** from the **Main Menu** bar. Tick the **Flash** and **HTML** boxes under the **Formats** tab. Use the same file names and locations as you did before – we'll overwrite the old **HTML** and **Flash** files.

 Click the **HTML** tab. Copy the settings from Figure 6.35. This time we'll specify the dimensions in **pixels** not **percent.**

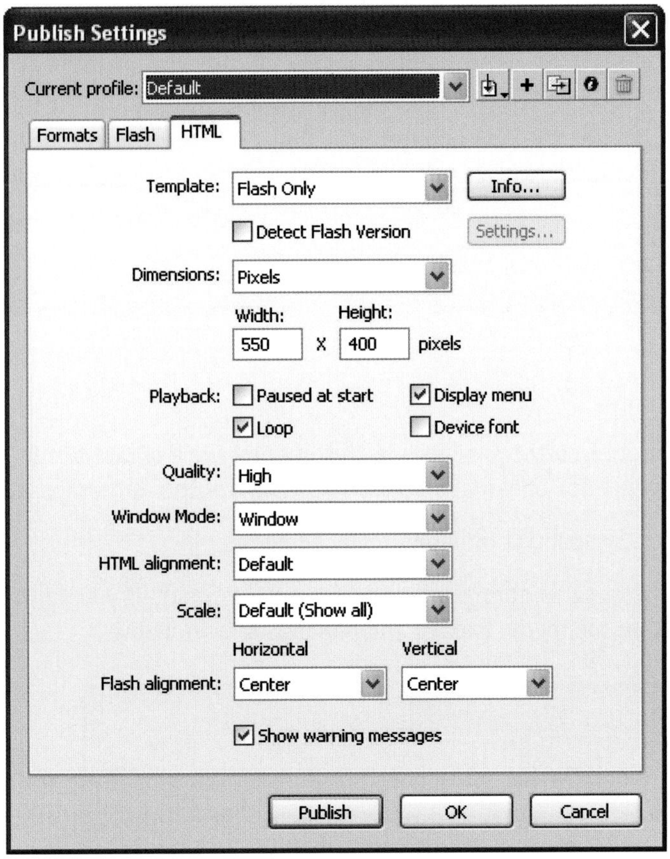

Figure 6.35: The Publish Settings window

 Click **Publish** then click **OK**.

 You can view the file by either opening the **HTML** file in an Internet browser, or simply pressing **Ctrl-Enter** whilst in **Flash** to preview the **.swf** file.

This time when you resize the browser window the picture doesn't resize with it, because the size was specified in **Pixels** not **Percent**.

 Close the browser window if you have one open.

 Press **Ctrl-S** to save your **Symbols.fla** file with its updated settings.

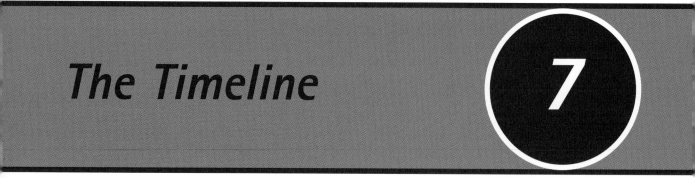

The Timeline

At last, an introduction to the **Timeline**! In this chapter we'll create a frame-by-frame animation of a rain cloud; it will not only move across the map, but the rain drops will move too!

You will need your **Symbols.fla** file open ready to begin.

○ The **Timeline** panel is normally located above the **Stage**. If you can't see it, select **Window**, **Timeline** from the menu. Expand the panel as shown below.

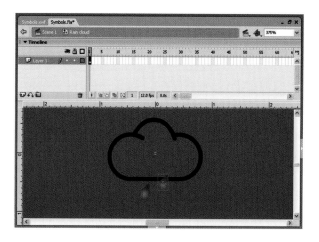

Figure 7.1: The Timeline panel appears above the Stage

The different parts of the **Timeline** are labelled below.

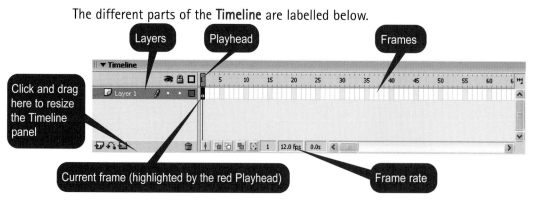

Figure 7.2: The Timeline panel

Frames

Frames in **Flash** are just like frames in a film or cartoon – something different is drawn in each frame and when the frames are put together in a sequence it looks as though the objects are moving. The frames in which you draw are called **keyframes**. It is normal to insert **regular frames** between **keyframes** in order to regulate the timing between the **keyframes**. The contents of a **keyframe** remain in view until the next **keyframe**.

For the **Rain cloud**, we will insert some **keyframes**, each having the rain droplets in a slightly different position.

Frame 1

Look at the **playhead**, highlighted in red. The **playhead** shows which frame you are viewing on the **Stage**. You are currently looking at **Frame 1**, which is the original **Rain cloud** symbol. **Frame 1** is a **keyframe** that is automatically inserted by **Flash**. By default, when you open a new **Flash** file, you work on **Frame 1**.

The **playhead** is shown in red. It will be at **Frame 1** by default when you start a new **Flash** file

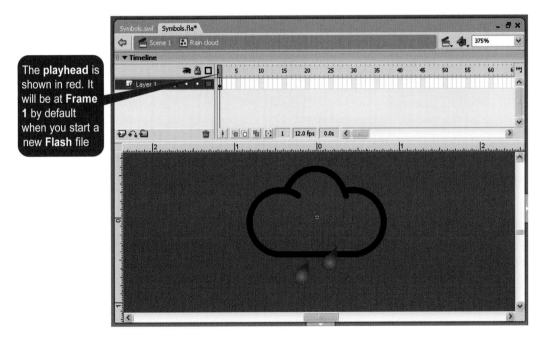

Figure 7.3

Inserting a keyframe

We need to insert another **keyframe**, and then change the raindrop positions.

◉   We will make **Frame 5** a **keyframe**. Right-click on **Frame 5** (see the screenshot below if you're not sure where to click) then select **Insert Keyframe** from the menu that appears.

> **Tip:** Selecting **Insert Keyframe** copies the contents of the last **keyframe** to the new **keyframe**. If you selected **Insert Blank Keyframe**, the contents wouldn't be copied and you'd have a blank **Stage**.

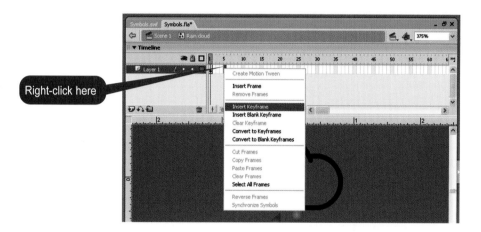

Figure 7.4: Inserting a keyframe

A circle appears in the frame to show that it is a **keyframe**. There is also a white square in **Frame 4**; this shows the end of the first **keyframe** sequence.

The red **playhead** has also moved to **Frame 5**, so the contents of **Frame 5** are currently displayed on the **Stage**. This will look identical to **Frame 1** because the content from the previous **keyframe** is always copied across to a new frame.

Using rulers and guidelines

We'll use guidelines to mark the position of the raindrops in **Frame 1** so that it is easier for us to return the raindrops to that position at the end of the animation sequence. By doing this, the animation can loop smoothly.

- If you can't already see the rulers, select **View, Rulers** from the **Main Menu** bar.

- To get a horizontal guideline, you have to click somewhere in the ruler at the top of the **Stage** then drag the guide onto the **Stage**. Try dragging a guide onto the **Stage** – we'll reposition it in a minute.

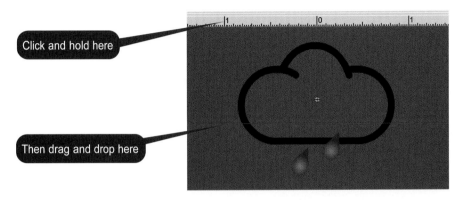

Figure 7.5: Adding a guideline

- Reposition the guideline by clicking and dragging it with the **Selection** tool. Position the guideline level with the top of the right-hand raindrop.

- Repeat this to get another guideline. Position it to be level with the top of the left-hand raindrop.

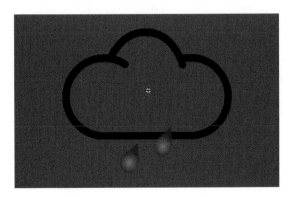

Figure 7.6: Guidelines positioned at the tops of the raindrops

Moving the raindrops

> Deselect everything by clicking away from the cloud and the guides. Click on the left-hand raindrop with the **Selection** tool.

> Press the down-arrow key **5 times**.

> Now select the right-hand raindrop. Again, press the down-arrow key **5 times**.

Inserting another keyframe

> Right-click in **Frame 10** then select **Insert Keyframe** from the menu that appears.

> Make sure that the **playhead** is in **Frame 10**. Select each raindrop in turn and press the down-arrow key **5 times** for each, just like you did before.

> Insert a **keyframe** in **Frame 15** and move the raindrops again.

Inserting another guide

> Click and drag another guide to mark the bottom of the left-hand raindrop.

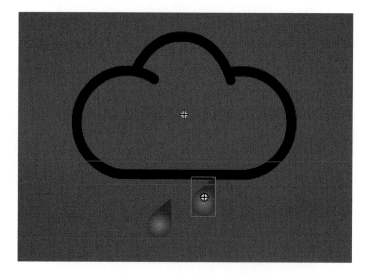

Figure 7.7

> Insert another **keyframe** in **Frame 20**. This time select the left-hand raindrop and press the up arrow key until it reaches the highest guide.

We want the raindrop to disappear for one **keyframe** when it hits the lowest guide.

▶   With the left-hand droplet selected, choose **Edit, Cut** from the **Main Menu** bar.

▶   Select the right-hand raindrop and press the down-arrow key **5 times.**

Frame 25

▶   Insert another **keyframe** in **Frame 25.** Move the right-hand drop down by **5** key presses.

▶   To re-insert the left-hand raindrop, select **Edit, Paste in Place** from the **Main Menu** bar.

Figure 7.8

▶   Insert another **keyframe** in **Frame 30** and move the raindrops down **5** key presses again. Repeat this until the right-hand raindrop touches the lowest guideline, which will be at about **Frame 40.** Add one final **keyframe** in **Frame 45** in which the right-hand raindrop disappears (and the left-hand raindrop moves down **5** key presses). You don't need to reinsert the deleted raindrop because it will reappear in **Frame 1.**

▶   Press **Ctrl-S** to save.

Removing the guides

▶   Remove the guides by clicking and dragging them up to the ruler at the top of the **Stage.** Drop them in the ruler and they'll disappear.

Scrubbing

There is a technique called **scrubbing** that you can use to easily preview your animation. It simply means dragging the **playhead** through the frames; each of the frames will then be shown on the **Stage** in turn.

○ Click and drag the red **playhead** in the **Timeline** panel through all the frames. Be careful to click and drag the top part of the **playhead** – don't click and drag in a frame.

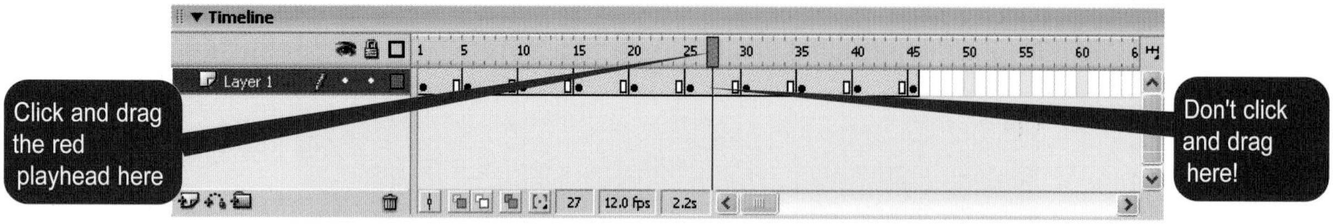

Figure 7.9: Scrubbing using the Timeline panel

Looping the animation

○ Select **Control** from the **Main Menu** bar. Make sure **Loop Playback** is ticked.

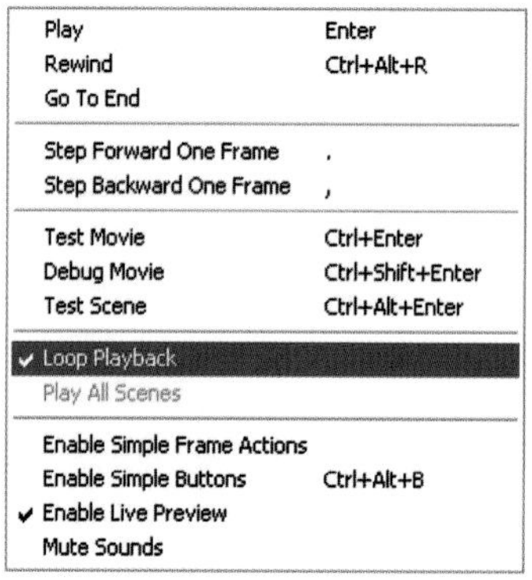

Figure 7.10: The Control menu

Playing the animation

○ Select **Control**, **Play** from the **Main Menu** bar. The animation will play on the **Stage** continuously.

○ Select **Control**, **Stop** from the **Main Menu** bar to stop the animation.

We will look at how to change the speed of the animation later in this chapter.

Tip: Instead of selecting **Control**, **Stop** from the menu, you can press **Escape** to stop the movie playing.

Frame view settings

You can change the way the frames in the **Timeline** panel are displayed.

❍ Click the **Frame view** icon at the top right of the **Timeline** panel.

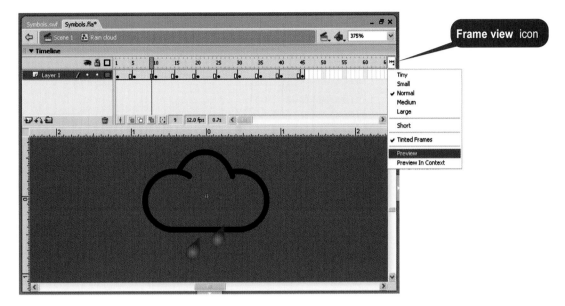

Figure 7.11: Frame view settings

❍ Select **Preview** from the menu that appears.

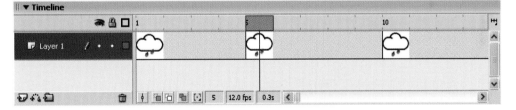

Figure 7.12: Using the Preview frame view setting

A small preview of each **keyframe** is now shown on the timeline.

❍ Return to normal view by clicking the **Frame view** icon then selecting **Normal** from the menu that appears.

Onion Skinning

This might seem like a strange name, but it comes from when illustrators drew each frame of an animation by hand. They would draw on a slightly translucent sheet (called an **onion skin**) so that they could see the previous frame through it. Onion skinning in **Flash** lets you view other frames whilst you're drawing the current frame.

▶ In the **Timeline** panel, click in **Frame 20**. At the bottom of the **Timeline** panel, click the **Onion Skin** icon marked in the screenshot below.

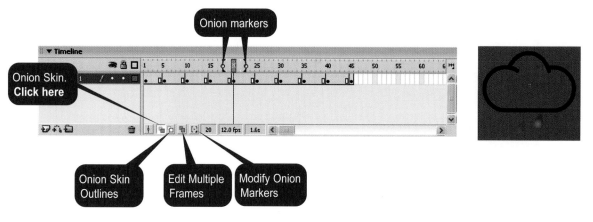

Figure 7.13

Some of the other frames are ghosted in.

▶ Click the **Modify Onion Markers** icon (marked in the above screenshot). Select **Onion All** from the menu.

▶ You can also click and drag the **onion markers** on the **Timeline** (they're labelled in the screenshot above). Try clicking and dragging them. The frames contained between the markers are the ones ghosted in on the **Stage**.

▶ Click the **Onion Skin Outlines** icon.

▶ When you've finished looking at the onion skin options, unclick all the icons.

Speeding up an animation

The animation is a bit slow. There are two ways in which we can speed it up:

❶   Edit the frame rate. However, this is not recommended. The frame rate should be left at the default of **12 fps** (frames per second), which is considered best for the Web and can be played on most computers.

❶   Delete some of the **regular frames** between **keyframes**. This is a better way of speeding up a movie.

We will experiment first with changing the **frame rate**.

▶   Select **Modify, Document** from the **Main Menu** bar.

▶   Change the **Frame rate** to **20 fps**. Click **OK**.

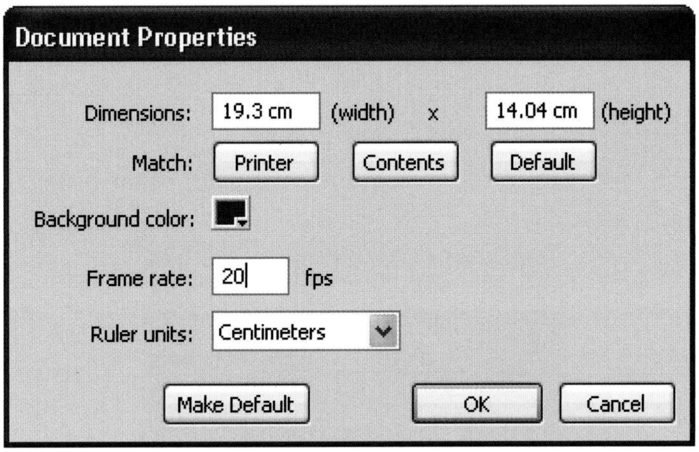

Figure 7.14: The Document Properties window

▶   Play the movie again by selecting **Control, Play** from the **Main Menu** bar; it should be a bit faster now.

▶   Change the frame rate back to **12 fps**.

We'll now use the second method to speed up the rain cloud, by deleting some of the **regular frames** between **keyframes**.

▶   Click on a **regular frame** between frames **1** and **5**. Right-click the frame then select **Remove Frames** from the menu that appears. Remove one **regular frame** from between each pair of **keyframes**.

▶   Play the movie again. If you want to speed it up more, just delete some more **regular frames**. You should delete the **regular frames** evenly, one from between each pair of **keyframes**, so that the animation runs at a constant speed.

Previewing the SWF file

To see the **Rain cloud** in a real document, we'll exit **Symbol edit** mode, drag a few **Rain cloud** instances onto the **Stage**, then do a **Publish Preview** of the page.

▶   Exit **Symbol edit** mode by clicking where it says **Scene 1** at the top of the **Stage**.

▶   Drag some instances of the **Rain cloud** symbol onto the **Stage** from the **Library** panel.

▶   Save the file.

▶   Press **Ctrl-Enter** to preview the **.swf** file.

It doesn't work! There is a good reason for this. Remember that when we created the **Rain cloud** symbol we set its behaviour to **Graphic** (look back to Figure 6.21). We need to change this now to **Movie Clip** for the animation to work.

Changing symbol behaviour

▶   Go back to the **FLA** file by clicking the **Symbols.fla** tab at the top of the screen. In the **Library** panel, click the **Rain cloud** symbol once to select it.

▶   Click the small **Information** icon at the bottom left of the panel.

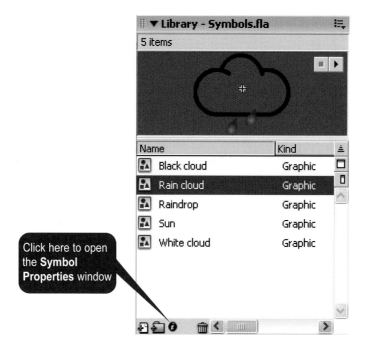

Click here to open the **Symbol Properties** window

Figure 7.15: The Library panel

The **Symbol Properties** window appears.

⊙ Change the behaviour to **Movie clip**.

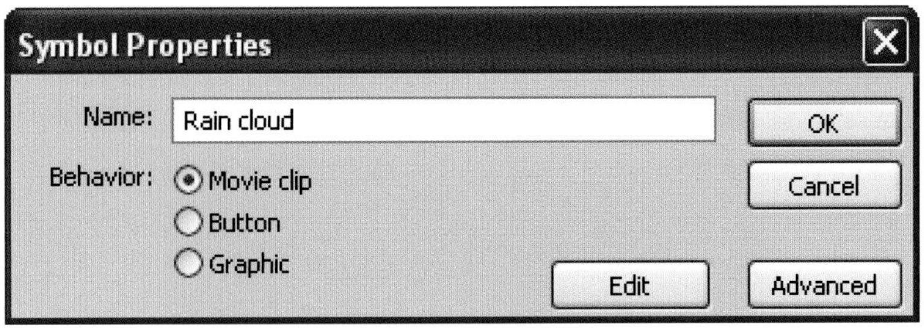

Figure 7.16: The Symbol Properties window

⊙ Click **OK**.

Although you have changed the behaviour of the symbol in the **Library** panel, the behaviour of the instances already on the **Stage** will not have changed. We'll look at this now.

⊙ With the **Selection** tool, click an instance of the **Rain cloud** on the **Stage**.

⊙ Take a look at the **Properties** panel.

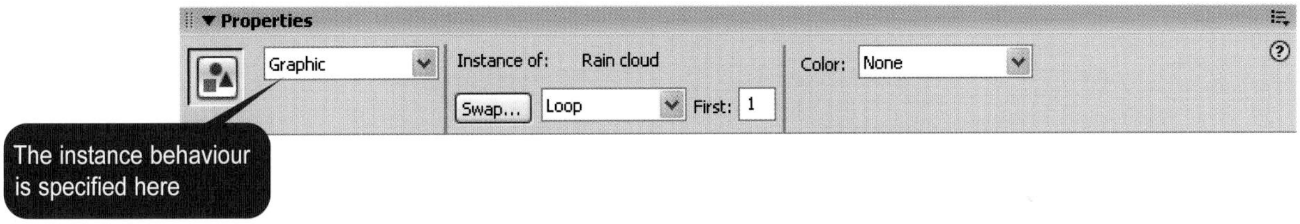

Figure 7.17: The Properties panel showing the properties of a Rain cloud symbol instance

⊙ The instance behaviour is still **Graphic**. Change this now to **Movie clip** by selecting it from the list in the **Properties** panel.

⊙ Leave the other instances as **Graphic**. Click and drag a couple more instances of the **Rain cloud** from the **Library** onto the **Stage**. Select them to view their properties; they should be **Movie Clips**.

⊙ Save the page by clicking **Ctrl-S**.

⊙ Now press **Ctrl-Enter** to preview the movie.

Some of the rain clouds will be moving and some of them will be still. The still ones are those for which the behaviour is still set to **Graphic**.

⊙ Save your file.

Creating and animating other weather symbols

As an exercise, try creating and animating some more weather symbols. You could try creating a lightning cloud with flashing lightning.

Start with a black cloud symbol and draw a lightning streak near it using the line tool. Then move it over the cloud and create a movie to make it flash.

Figure 7.18

Then try creating a snow cloud, which can also be based on the black cloud.

Figure 7.19

You can look at the MET office website at **www.met-office.gov.uk** and the BBC website **www.bbc.co.uk** to see what weather symbols they use.

If you need extra help, more detailed instructions are available on the website **www.payne-gallway.co.uk** in the Student Resources section for this book.

Store your symbols in the **Library** of the **Symbols** file.

     Press **Ctrl-S** to save the file.

Organising the Library

You can organise the **Library** by creating different folders. We'll create one to put all the symbols in.

○ In the **Library** panel, click the **Add New Folder** icon at the bottom. Enter **Weather symbols** as the folder name, then press **Enter**.

○ Now click and drag each of the weather symbols and drop them onto the new folder.

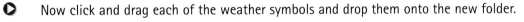

▼ Library – Weather map.fla		
10 items		
Name	**Kind**	**U:**
Black cloud	Graphic	
FOG	Graphic	
Lightning cloud	Movie Clip	
Rain cloud	Movie Clip	
Raindrop	Graphic	
Snow cloud	Movie Clip	
Snowflake	Movie Clip	
Sun	Graphic	
Weather symbols	Folder	
White cloud	Graphic	

▼ Library – Weather map.fla		
10 items		
Name	**Kind**	
Weather symbols	Folder	

Figure 7.20: The Library panel

○ Close the **Symbols.fla** and **Symbols.swf** files; say **Yes** if prompted to save.

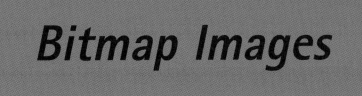

Bitmap Images

In this chapter we will create the map of Britain that will become the basis of the weather map. We will start by importing a bitmap image. We will then convert the bitmap image to a vector image to make it easier to edit.

Copying an image from a web site

We will copy a map from a website – there's no point spending ages creating your own when there are so many free resources available on the Web.

> **Tip:** You should be aware of copyright laws when using other people's material – if you intend to use it for anything other than your own practice projects you must ask permission.

- ◗ Create a new **Flash** document either using the **Start page** or by selecting **File, New** from the **Main Menu** bar.

- ◗ Set the background colour of the **Stage** to blue using the **Properties** panel.

- ◗ Open **Internet Explorer** or any other web browser. Go to **www.payne-gallway.co.uk/ flash/map**. There is a map here; right-click on it with the mouse.

- ◗ Select **Copy** from the shortcut menu that appears. This map has now been copied to the clipboard.

Figure 8.1: The map on the Payne-Gallway website

○ Return to **Flash**. Select **Edit, Paste in Centre** from the **Main Menu** bar.

The map is pasted onto the **Stage**. Don't worry that it is a bit big – we'll resize it.

○ In the **Zoom** menu at the top right of the **Stage**, select **Show All**. The whole map should now be in view.

Resizing an imported image

 ○ Use the **Free Transform** tool to resize the image. You'll need to use the **Scale** option at the bottom of the **Toolbox**.

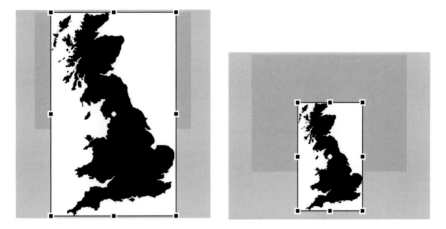

Figure 8.2: Resizing the map to fit on the Stage

○ Now move the pointer over the map so that it becomes a crossed arrow. Click and drag the map to the centre of the canvas. Select **Show All** again from the **Zoom** menu.

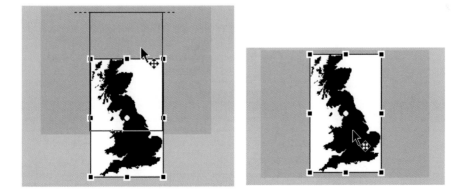

Figure 8.3

Converting bitmap images to vector images

The imported image is a bitmap image. It will be much easier to work on, and will take up less file space, if it is a vector image. As a bitmap image, **Flash** cannot distinguish between the white background and the black land. We want to be able select them separately so that we can delete the white background.

○ Click the **Selection** tool. Make sure the whole map is selected. Choose **Modify, Bitmap, Trace Bitmap** from the **Main Menu** bar.

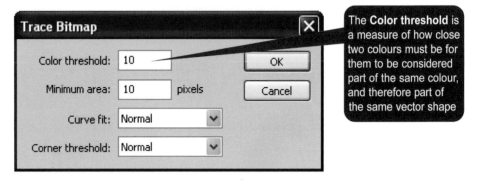

The **Color threshold** is a measure of how close two colours must be for them to be considered part of the same colour, and therefore part of the same vector shape

Figure 8.4: The Trace Bitmap window

○ Copy the settings above for the **Trace Bitmap** window. Click **OK**.

Figure 8.5: Bitmap converted to vectors, with everything selected

○ Click away from the map to deselect everything. Now click on the white background to select it, then press the **Delete** key.

○ Choose **Edit, Select All** from the **Main Menu** bar. Change the map colour to **green** using the **Properties** panel.

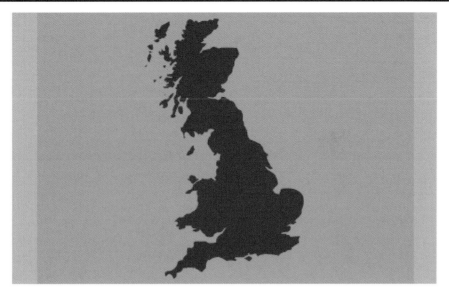

Figure 8.6: The green map with the white background removed

The white background has been deleted! That looks much neater.

Grouping the map

The map consists of many small islands. We need to group the map so that when we move it we don't separate the mainland from the islands!

 With the whole map still selected, choose **Modify, Group** from the **Main Menu** bar.

Deleting a symbol

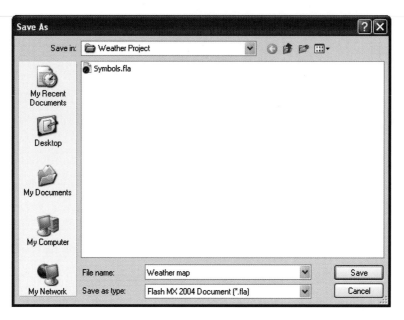

- Open the **Library** panel if it is not already open. You'll find that the bitmap image has been added as a symbol. Delete this by clicking it in the **Library** panel then pressing the **Delete** icon at the bottom of the panel. Click **Yes** to confirm deletion.

- Select **File, Save** from the **Main Menu** bar.

Figure 8.7: Save As window

- Locate the **Weather Project** folder. Save the file as **Weather map.fla**.

Importing Library symbols from another file

Notice that the **Library** is empty. Were you expecting to see all your weather symbols there? The weather symbols are part of the **Library** for the **Symbols.fla** file. We'll have to import those symbols to the **Weather map's** own **Library**.

There are two ways to share symbols across files:

One way is called **runtime sharing**. With runtime sharing the symbols are stored only once, in a shared file. If a symbol is updated, the change affects all files sharing that symbol. The shared file is given a URL and must be made available when the **Flash** movie is run. This can get a bit confusing!

The other way is literally to copy the symbols across from one file to another. The symbols are saved twice. If a symbol is modified in one file it will not affect the symbol copy in the other file. We will use this method.

- We need to open the **Symbols.fla** file to copy the symbols across. Open it by selecting **File, Open Recent**, then clicking **Symbols.fla** in the list.

Notice that a second **Library** panel has appeared, for the **Symbols** file, called **Library –
Symbols.fla**.

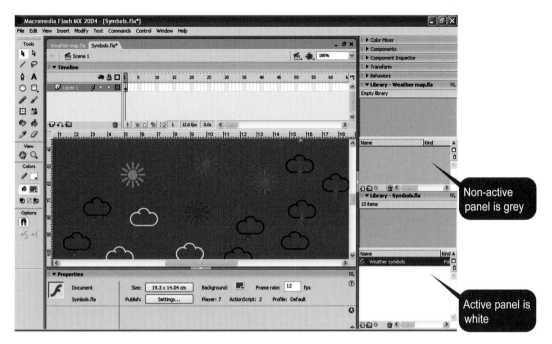

Figure 8.8: The Library panels from both documents are visible

The **Library** for the **Weather map** is shaded grey because **Symbols** is the active file. (The top
panel for each **Library** is also grey, because no symbols are being previewed.)

    Click the page tab for the **Weather map** file (above the **Timeline** panel). Notice that now
it's the **Library – Symbols** panel that's shaded grey.

    Click the **Weather symbols** folder in the **Library – Symbols** panel.

    Now click and drag the folder to where it says **Name** in the **Library – Weather map**
panel.

All the symbols are copied across!

    Close the **Symbols.fla** file without saving.

Add symbols to Frame 1

- Expand the **Timeline** panel if it isn't already visible. The red playhead will be on **Frame 1**; you are already looking at **Frame 1**.

- Double-click the **Weather symbols** folder (the icon, not the name) in the **Library** panel to expand it. Click and drag some weather symbols onto the map from the **Library** panel. You could even try to make your weather accurate by checking the Met Office website first (**www.met–office.gov.uk**).

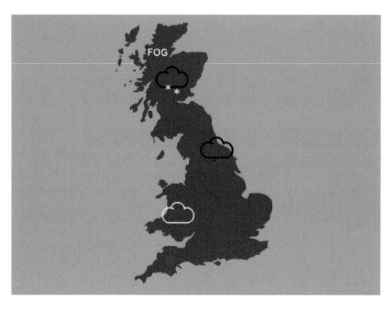

Figure 8.9: Adding symbols to the map

- Save the **Weather map.fla** file. Preview the file by pressing **Ctrl-Enter**.

- Close the **Weather map.swf** file. Close the **Weather map.fla** file if this is the end of a session.

In the next chapter we'll start animating the symbols across the map.

Layers and Tweened Animation

In this chapter we'll cover how to use **tweening** (automatically generating a smooth transition between **keyframes**) to move the weather symbols across the map.

Layers

In order to use **tweening**, each symbol must be on a different **layer**. You have probably come across **layers** in other graphics software. In **Flash**, **layers** can be used in the traditional way, to arrange the order of objects on the **Stage** and allow them to be manipulated independently. The main use for **layers** in **Flash** is to organise animations: Each piece of an animation is placed on a separate layer.

○ Open the **Weather map.fla** file.

The **layers** are shown in the **Timeline** panel. At the moment there is just one layer, called **Layer 1**.

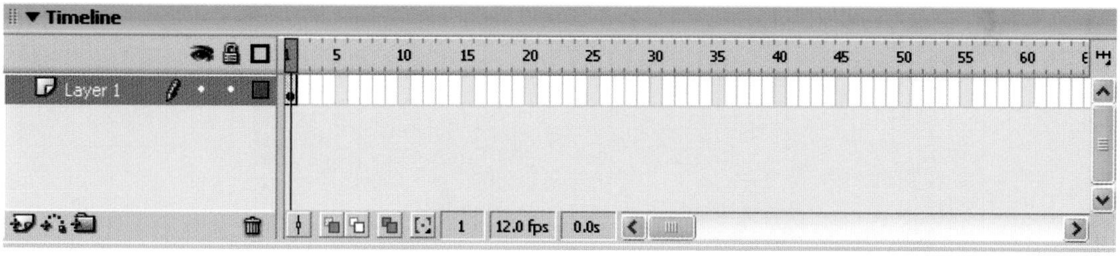

Figure 9.1: The Timeline panel

The first job is to place each symbol currently on the map on a different layer.

○ Right-click a **Sun** symbol on the **Stage** (add one from the **Library** if necessary). Select **Distribute to Layers** from the menu that appears.

It looks as though the symbol has disappeared! Look at the **Timeline** panel. There is now another layer called **Sun**; the layer has automatically been named after the symbol.

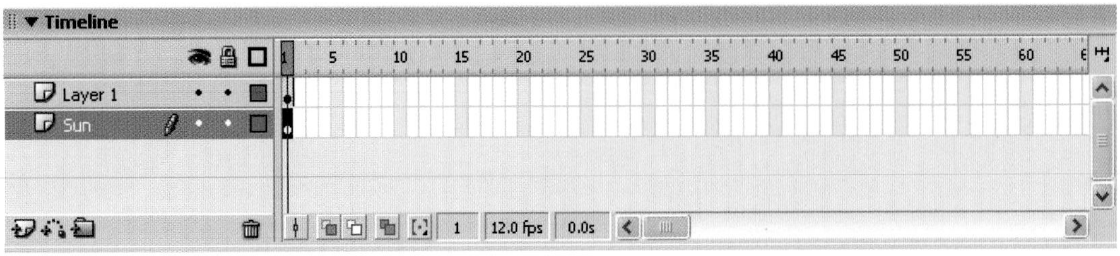

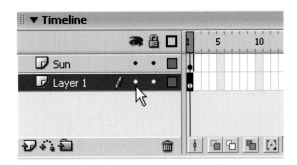

Figure 9.2: The Sun symbol is placed on its own layer

Layer order

The reason the **Sun** has disappeared is because the **Sun** layer is below **Layer 1**, so it is hidden under the green map.

     Click and drag the **Sun** layer in the **Timeline** panel to be above **Layer 1**. The sun reappears on the map.

Other layer options

We'll just go through some of the icons and what they do.

Hiding and showing layers

     Click to select **Layer 1** in the **Timeline** panel. Click the small dot under the eye icon (see screenshot below).

Figure 9.3: Hiding a layer

This hides **Layer 1**, leaving only the **Sun** symbol in the **Sun** layer visible.

Figure 9.4: The green map on Layer 1 is hidden

○   Click again in the same place to unhide **Layer 1**.

Locking a layer

   ○   With **Layer 1** still selected, click below the padlock icon in the **Timeline** panel.

○   Now try to select something in **Layer 1** (at the moment everything is in **Layer 1** except the **Sun** symbol). You can't, because it is locked. Now unlock the layer by clicking in the same place in the **Timeline** panel.

Layer outline

○   Click the square symbol on the right of the **Lock** symbol; all the objects in that layer are shown as outlines. Click again to restore the fills.

Distribute all symbols to layers

○   First of all, to simplify things, delete some of the symbols on the **Stage** so you only have one of each type of symbol. You can add more later.

○   Deselect everything by pressing the **Escape** key. Select all the remaining symbols – not the **Sun** or the map itself – using the **Selection** tool (hold down the **Shift** key to select multiple symbols). Right-click one of the symbols and select **Distribute to Layers**.

There are now many layers in the **Timeline** panel, each with a different symbol.

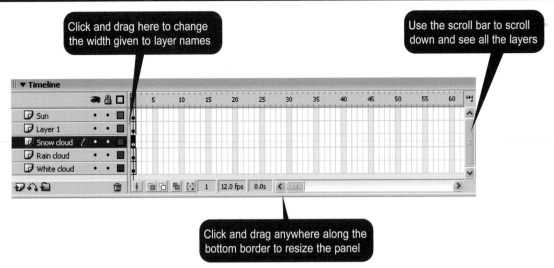

Figure 9.5: Distributing all the symbols to a different layer

▶ Click and drag **Layer 1** to the bottom of the layers so that the green map sits behind all the symbols.

Renaming layers

▶ Double-click where it says **Layer 1** in the **Timeline** panel. Type **Map background** then press **Enter**.

▶ Lock the **Map background** layer by clicking below the padlock symbol in the **Timeline** panel.

The other layers will probably have been named after the symbols, so you don't need to rename these.

Motion tweening

With motion tweening, you don't have to enter the position of objects in every frame; you simply specify where you want the object in **Frame 1**, then in another frame (say **Frame 100** for this example) and **Flash** will animate the object smoothly from one frame to the other.

▶ Insert a **keyframe** in **Frame 100** of the **Sun** layer (to do this, right-click **Frame 100**, then select **Insert Keyframe** from the menu that appears).

The **Stage** is now displaying **Frame 100**.

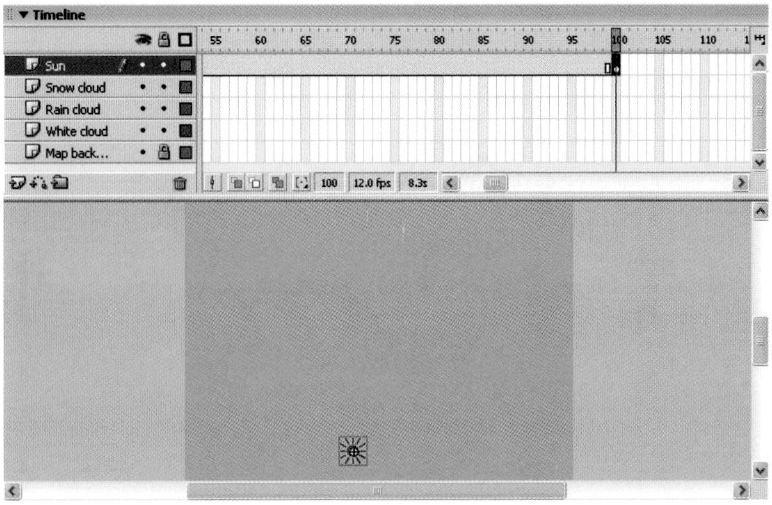

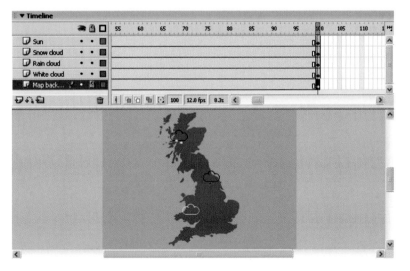

Figure 9.6: The Stage at Frame 100

The green map has disappeared! This is because there is no **Frame 100** in the **Map background** layer. The green background exists in only **Frame 1**.

In the **Timeline** panel, insert a **keyframe** in **Frame 100** in the **Map background** layer.

The green map reappears.

Now insert a **keyframe** in **Frame 100** for all the other layers. The shortcut to inserting a **keyframe** is to click in **Frame 100** then press the **F6** key.

Figure 9.7

Click **Frame 100** in the **Sun** layer in the **Timeline** panel. Click the **Selection** tool then click the **Sun** symbol. For you to select the sun, you must have only the **keyframe** in **Frame 100** selected. If you have a **regular** frame selected, or more than one frame selected, it won't work.

◉   Now click and drag the sun across the map.

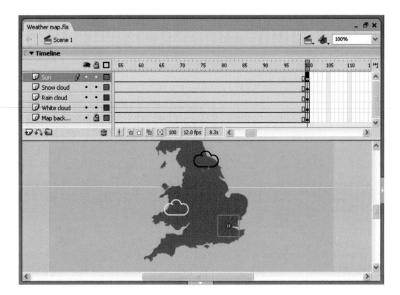

Figure 9.8: Selecting the Sun symbol

◉   Test the movie by selecting **Control, Play** from the **Main Menu** bar. Press the **Escape** key or select **Control, Stop** to stop the movie.

The sun doesn't move smoothly across the map; it stays in its initial location until **Frame 100** when it jumps to its new position. This is because we haven't created a **motion tween** between **Frame 1** and **Frame 100**.

◉   Right-click somewhere in the **Sun** layer in a **regular frame** (not a **keyframe**) between **Frame 1** and **Frame 100**.

◉   Select **Create Motion Tween** from the menu that appears.

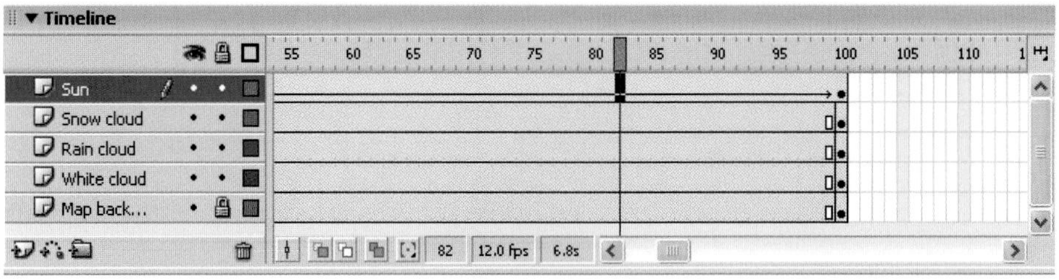

Figure 9.9: Creating a motion tween between two keyframes

A long arrow appears between **Frame 1** and **Frame 100** to represent the **motion tween**.

> **Tip:** If you ever get a broken line representing the **tween**, that means there's something wrong and **Flash** hasn't been able to successfully calculate the **tween**.

○ Now test the movie again by selecting **Control, Play** from the menu. The sun moves smoothly across the map. Note that the movie will play from where the **playhead** is currently positioned. Try clicking **Frame 1** before playing the movie.

Adding rotation

We can make the sun rotate as it moves across the map.

○ Select **Frame 100**. Select the **Sun**, then click the **Free Transform** tool in the **Toolbox**.

○ Hold the mouse near a corner node so that the mouse pointer changes to the rotation icon. Click and drag to rotate the sun; rotate it **180** degrees (holding down **Shift** makes this easier).

○ Test the movie again. The sun looks like it's rolling across the country!

> **Tip:** You can control the direction of the rotation by changing the value of the **Rotate** setting in the **Properties** panel (**CW** for clockwise, **CCW** for counter-clockwise).

Resizing

○ Select **Frame 100** in the **Sun** layer. With the **Free Transform** tool, select the sun then hold down the **Shift** key while you click and drag a corner node to make the symbol bigger.

○ Click the **Selection** tool. Deselect everything by clicking away from the map. Now click the **Sun** symbol in **Frame 100**. In the **Properties** panel, change the colour to a **Tint**. Give the **Sun** a reddish tint.

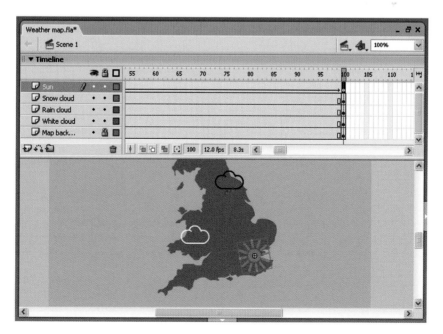

Figure 9.10

- ◐ Select **Control**, **Loop Playback** from the **Main Menu** bar.

- ◐ Save the page, then preview the movie by pressing **Ctrl-Enter**. The sun gradually gets bigger and changes colour.

Guide layers

At the moment, the sun moves in a straight line between the positions you specify in **Frame 1** and **Frame 100**. It is possible to specify a more complex path for the sun between the two positions; this is done with a **guide layer**.

Creating a guide layer

You can either create a normal layer, then turn it into a guide layer, or you can just create a guide layer to begin with; we'll do the latter.

- ◐ Click on the **Sun** layer. At the bottom of the **Timeline** panel, click the **Add Guide Layer** icon.

A new layer called **Guide: Sun** appears. The **Sun** layer has been indented to show that it is attached to the guide layer above.

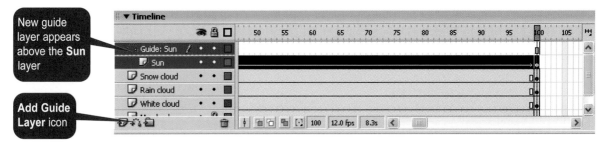

Figure 9.11: Adding a guide layer attached to the Sun layer

Drawing a guide line

Now we'll draw a line to represent the path that the sun must follow.

- ◐ Click in **Frame 1** in the **Guide** layer. Click the **Pencil** tool in the **Toolbox**. At the bottom of the **Toolbox**, select the **Smooth** option.

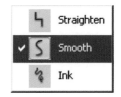

Figure 9.12: Pencil tool options in the Toolbox

○ With the **Pencil** tool, draw a curved line that starts approximately where the **Sun** is in **Frame 1**, and ends where the **Sun** is in **Frame 100**. You won't actually be able to see the position of the sun in **Frame 100** while you draw this, but don't worry if it isn't very close; we can adjust it in a minute.

Figure 9.13: Drawing a guideline using the Pencil tool

At the moment, this won't work. The guide line has to be positioned exactly at the centrepoint of the sun at its start and finish positions. To reposition it, we will use the **Selection** tool together with the **Snap** option.

○ Click **Frame 1** in the **Guide** layer. Zoom in on the **Sun** symbol and the start of the guide line. Now click the **Selection** tool in the **Toolbox**, then click the **Snap** option (the magnet icon) at the bottom of the **Toolbox**.

○ Press the **Escape** key to deselect everything. Make sure you are in **Frame 1** in the **Guide** layer. Hover the pointer over the end of the guide line; now click and drag the end of the line to the centre of the **Sun** then drop it. It should snap to the centre.

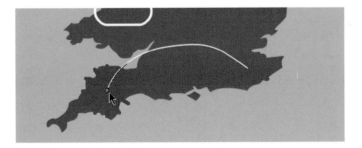

Figure 9.14: Snapping the guideline to the centre of the Sun symbol

○ Now select **Frame 100** in the **Timeline** panel. Deselect everything by pressing **Escape** then click and drag the sun so that it snaps to the end of the line.

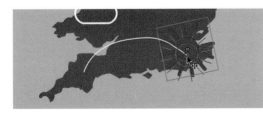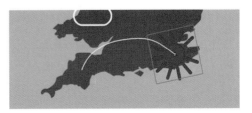

Figure 9.15: Snapping the guideline to the centre of the Sun symbol

○ Click and drag the red **playhead** over the frames to preview the animation – the sun should now follow the guideline!

> **Tip:** If your sun doesn't follow the guideline, you may not have snapped the end of the guideline exactly onto the sun.

Hiding the Guide layer

You don't want this line to be visible now, so we'll just hide the guide layer. You will be able to unhide it at any time if you need to edit it.

 ○ In the **Timeline** panel, click the dot in the **Guide** layer under the eye symbol. A red cross will appear to show that the layer is hidden, and the line should disappear from the **Stage**.

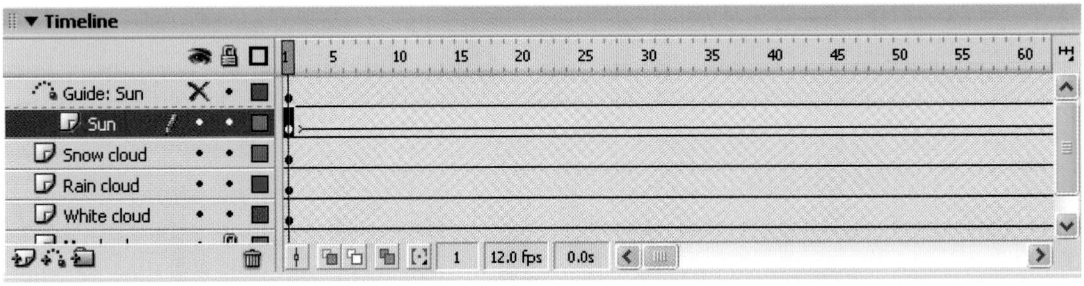

Figure 9.16: Hiding the Guide layer in the Timeline panel

Time to take a break!

○ Save your file, and close it if this is the end of a session.

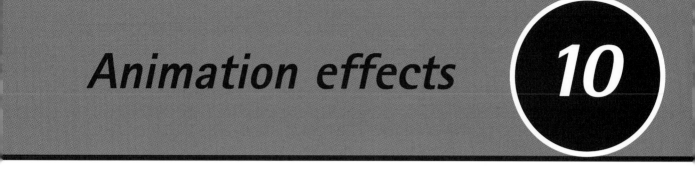

Animation effects 10

You can add many different effects to your animations. We'll look at a few of them in this chapter – you may prefer to skip these until you need them in your own project!

 Open the **Weather map.fla** file if it is not already open.

Fading symbols in and out

You can fade a symbol in or out by changing its **Alpha** value in the **Properties** panel. We will make the **Rain cloud** symbol gradually disappear.

 Move the red **playhead** to **Frame 100** in the **Timeline** panel.

● Click the **Rain cloud** symbol on the map with the **Selection** tool. In the **Properties** panel select **Alpha** from the **Color** list. Enter **0%** as the **Alpha** value.

▼ Properties			
[icon]	Movie Clip ⌄	Instance of: Rain cloud	Color: Alpha ⌄ 0% ⌄
	<Instance Name>	Swap...	
W: 46.3 X: 282.6			
H: 39.0 Y: 175.8			

Figure 10.1: Changing the Alpha value in the Properties panel

● Preview the animation by clicking and dragging the red **playhead** across the frames. Notice that the **Rain cloud** symbol doesn't fade nicely – it just disappears in **Frame 100**!

We need to add a **motion tween** to make the symbol fade gradually. Even though we are not using motion, adding a **motion tween** will smooth the transition between **Frame 1** and **Frame 100**.

● Right-click a **regular frame** between **Frame 1** and **Frame 100** in the **Rain cloud** layer. Select **Create Motion Tween** from the menu that appears.

● Now test the animation by selecting **Control, Play** from the **Main Menu** bar. Press **Escape** to stop playing the animation.

The **Rain cloud** symbol should now fade gradually. We will move the end **keyframe** to **Frame 50** so that the rain fades by **Frame 50** and then remains invisible until **Frame 100**.

Moving frames

- ◉   Click on **Frame 100** in the **Rain cloud** layer to select it. Now click and drag it to **Frame 50**, then drop it.

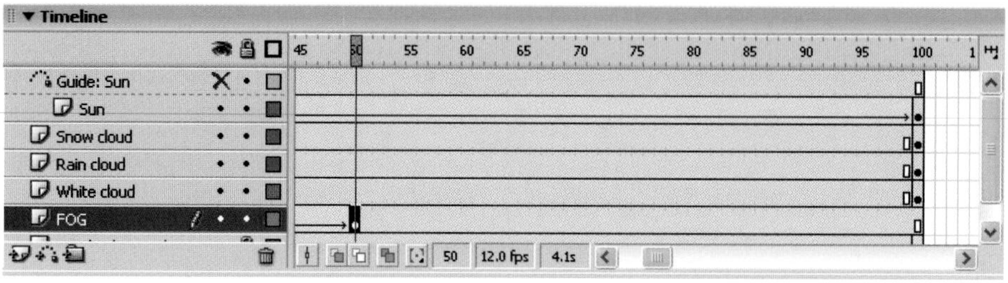

Figure 10.2: Moving frames in the Timeline panel

The **keyframe** moves to **Frame 50**. The small square in **Frame 100** means that the contents of **Keyframe 50** will remain until **Frame 100**; the symbol is actually invisible in **Frame 50** anyway, so this makes no difference. We can delete **Frames 51–100** in the **Rain cloud** layer.

Deleting frames

- ◉   Without first selecting it, click and drag from **Frame 100** to **Frame 51**. This should select all these frames.

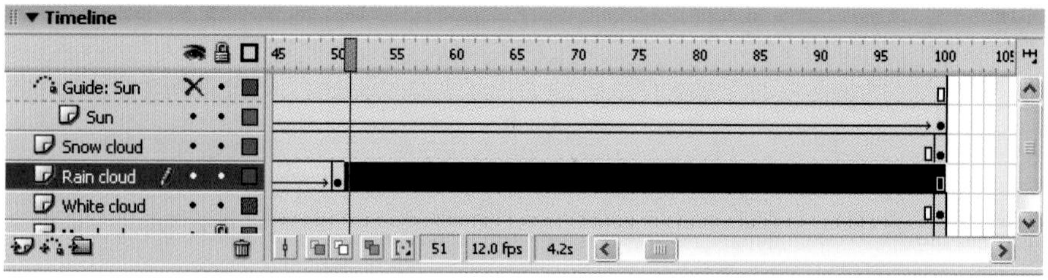

Figure 10.3: Deleting frames in the Timeline panel

- ◉   Right-click somewhere in the selection, and choose **Remove Frames** from the menu that appears.

- ◉   Save by pressing **Ctrl-S** or by selecting **File, Save** from the **Main Menu** bar.

Ease in and Ease out

When applying **motion tweening**, you can use the **Ease** property in the **Properties** panel to make motion start slowly and speed up, or the other way around. This can make your tweened animations look a bit less artificial.

○ Click in any frame in the **Sun** layer. In the **Properties** panel, enter a value of ?60 in the **Ease** field. **Play** the animation to see the difference.

Timeline effects

Flash has inbuilt effects that you can easily add to your animation. Here, we'll look at the **'Drop Shadow'** Timeline effect.

'Drop Shadow' Timeline Effect

○ Select one of the symbols (not the white cloud) in **Frame 1** with the **Selection** tool. In the **Timeline** panel make sure just **Frame 1** is selected, not the whole layer. Go to **Insert**, **Timeline Effects, Effects, Drop Shadow** on the **Main Menu** bar.

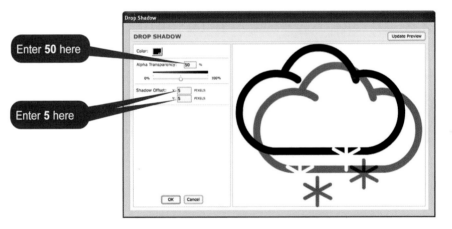

Figure 10.4: The 'Drop Shadow' Timeline effect

○ Enter the settings shown in Figure 10.4. Click the **Update Preview** button to view the changes. Click **OK** when you're happy.

The shadow appears on the map behind the symbol. Notice that the **drop shadow** appears as a separate symbol in the **Library** panel called **Drop Shadow 1**.The layer name in the **Timeline** panel has changed to the new symbol name **Drop Shadow 1**. There is also a new folder in the **Library** panel, called **Effects**, where all of the symbols used in the **Timeline effect** are added.

○ To edit the effect, right-click the symbol on the **Stage**, then select **Timeline Effects, Edit Effect** from the menu that appears.

Transition Timeline effect

The 'Transition' Timeline effect can be used to change the way a symbol appears on or disappears from the **Stage**. We will use it to fade a symbol in and out; we did this earlier by changing the **Alpha** property in the **Properties** panel, but this is a much easier way to achieve the same result.

○ First, if you don't already have a **Black cloud** on the **Stage**, drag an instance of the **Black cloud** symbol onto the **Stage** in **Frame 1**. Right-click the symbol, then select **Distribute to Layers** from the menu that appears.

○ Click the **Black cloud** symbol, then click **Frame 1** of the **Black cloud** layer in the **Timeline** panel. Select **Insert, Timeline Effects, Transform/Transition, Transition** from the **Main Menu** bar.

○ Copy the settings given in Figure 10.5, then click **OK**.

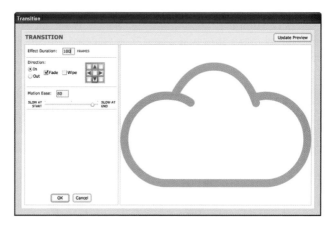

Figure 10.5: The Transition Timeline Effect

○ Preview the effect by pressing **Ctrl-Enter**.

Other Timeline effects

 Try out some of the other **Timeline effects** with the other symbols.

Removing a Timeline effect

 To remove a **Timeline effect** from a symbol, first select the symbol, then choose **Modify**, **Timeline Effects**, **Remove Effect** from the **Main Menu** bar.

Publishing the map

Have a look at what the map will look like in an Internet browser by publishing it.

 Select **File**, **Publish Settings** from the **Main Menu** bar.

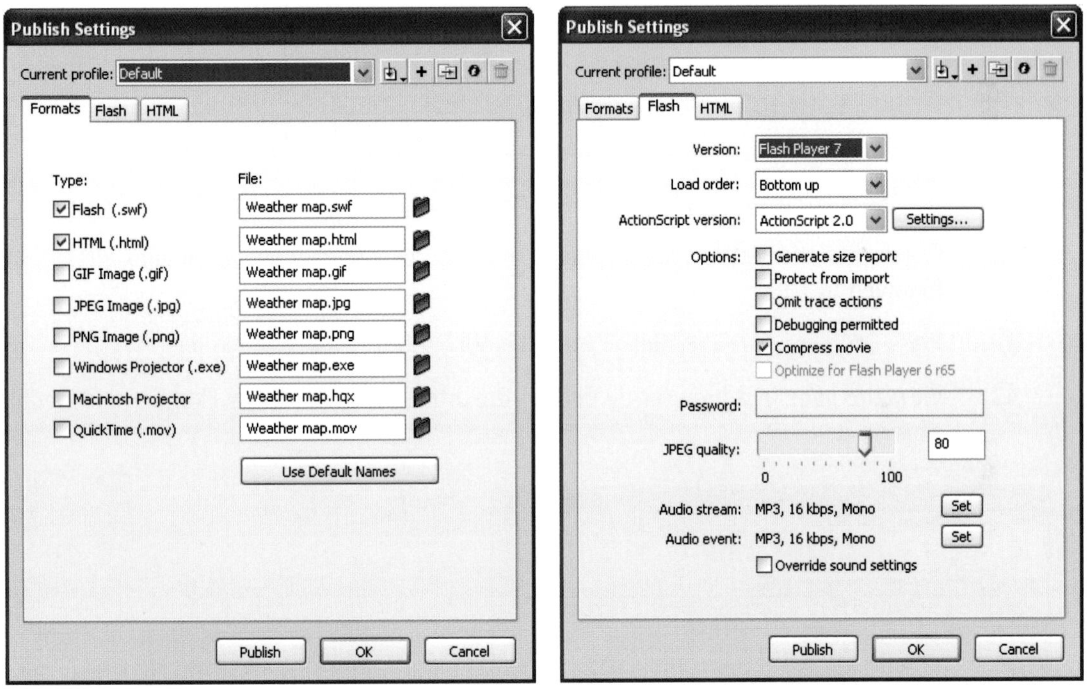

Figure 10.6: The Publish Settings window – Formats and Flash

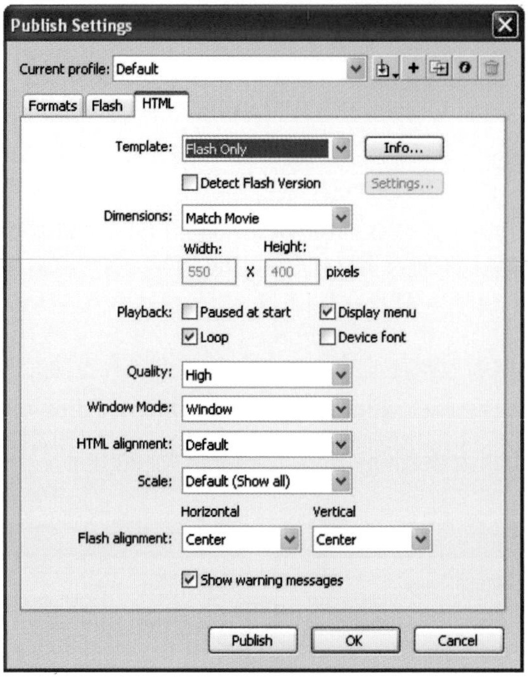

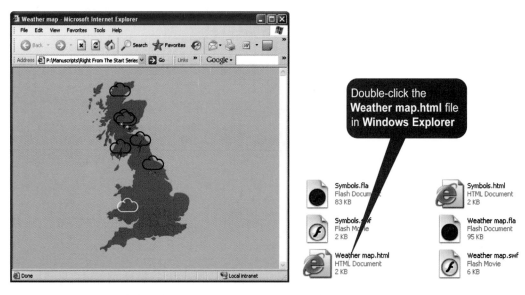

Figure 10.7: The Publish Settings window – HTML

◉ Check that the settings are as shown in the screenshots above, then click **Publish** followed by **OK**.

◉ Press **Ctrl-S** to save the file.

◉ View the page in a browser by finding the **.html** file in **Windows Explorer** and double-clicking it.

Figure 10.8: Viewing the published HTML file in Internet Explorer

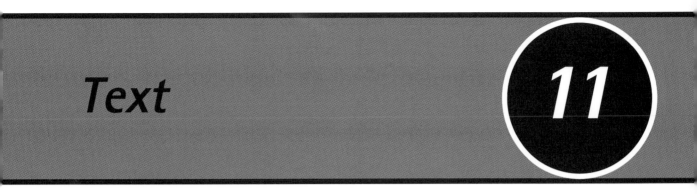

Text

In **Flash**, text can be entered in text labels or boxes, edited, formatted, manipulated and even used to create animations. We will introduce some of the text functions by creating a **fog** symbol which just consists of the word **fog**. We'll look at paragraph text later in the book.

○ Open the **Weather map.fla** file if it is not already open.

 ○ Click the **Text** tool in the **Toolbox**. Make sure you have nothing selected, then have a look at the **Properties** panel.

Figure 11.1: The Properties panel showing Text tool properties

○ Copy the settings from in the screenshot above – notice the text is Arial size 12, white, and left-aligned.

○ Click once on a blank part of the **Stage**.

Figure 11.2

○ Now type **FOG**. The text will appear grey rather than white – this is just so that you can see it against the white background of the text box.

○ Click away from the text box to deselect it.

Editing text

 Click and drag the cursor across the text **FOG** to select it. In the **Properties** panel type **14** as the font size then press **Enter**. You can change any other properties too, if you wish, whilst the text is selected.

 Click away from the text to deselect it.

Moving text

You can move text just like you would move a shape.

 Click the **Selection** tool in the **Toolbox**, then click the text.

Figure 11.3

A blue box appears around the text – just like it does for the other shapes you've created and turned into **Overlay level** objects. Text automatically becomes and **Overlay level** object.

 Click and drag the text across the **Stage**.

Rotating and resizing text

You can rotate and resize text using the **Free Transform** tool.

 Click the **Free Transform** tool in the **Toolbox**, then click the text to select it (if it is not already selected).

 Try rotating and resizing the text.

Figure 11.4: Resizing and rotating text

Reshaping text

There are a couple of the **Free Transform** tool options greyed-out at the moment because they can only be applied to graphical shapes. In order to turn text into a graphical shape, you have to 'break it apart'.

 With the text selected, select **Modify, Break Apart** from the **Main Menu** bar.

Figure 11.5: Breaking Apart text

The word has been broken up so that each letter has its own text box. The letters can still be edited as text.

 With the **Selection** tool, first deselect everything, then click on one of the letters.

 Select **Modify, Break Apart** again from the **Main Menu** bar.

The letter is now a graphical shape and can be manipulated just like a circle or square. It can no longer be edited as text.

 Click it with the **Selection** tool to select it then move it around the **Stage**. Try reshaping it using the **Free Transform** tool.

Figure 11.6: The Properties panel showing Text tool properties

 Select all the letters and delete them.

○ Use the **Text** tool with the same initial settings (**Arial**, size **14**) to write **FOG** again.

Figure 11.7

Turning text into a symbol

You create a symbol from text in just the same way as from graphical objects.

○ Select the text with the **Selection** tool. Choose **Modify, Convert to Symbol** from the **Main Menu** bar.

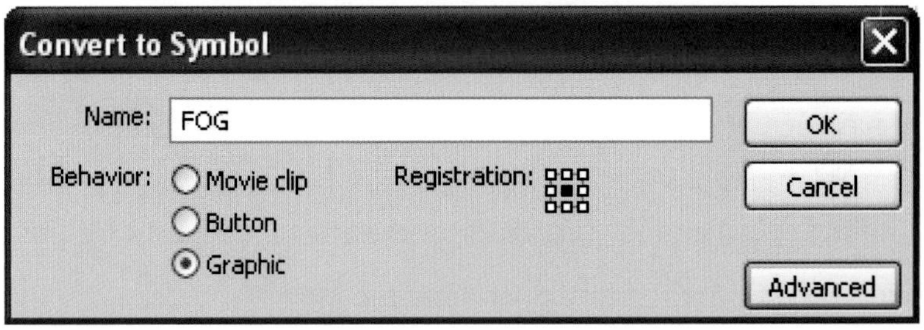

Figure 11.8: The Convert to Symbol window

○ Copy the settings from Figure 11.8. Click **OK**.

○ Tidy up the **Library** panel by dragging the new **FOG** symbol from the top level and dropping it into the **Weather symbols** folder.

○ Save the document.

Scrolling text

Now we'll add some scrolling text for a running commentary on the day's weather. To do this we will use a text box combined with a **Mask** layer.

 Right-click the **Map background** layer in the **Timeline** panel and select **Insert Layer** from the menu that appears. Rename the layer **Monday text**.

 Click in **Frame 1** of the new **Monday text** layer. Click the **Text** tool in the **Toolbox**. Click once on the **Stage** then press the **Escape** key. In the **Properties** panel, make the text Arial, 14 point, grey and left-aligned (see below).

Figure 11.9: The Properties panel showing Text tool properties

 Now click and drag out a text box to the right of the weather map.

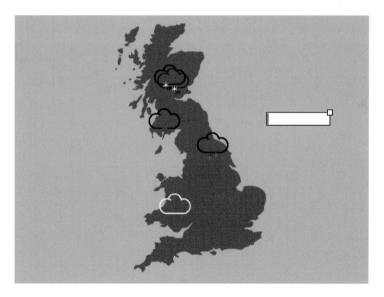

Figure 11.10

B ───●   Type in some text that matches your weather symbols. Add a **Monday** title at the top of the text box and make it bold by selecting it and clicking the **Bold** symbol in the **Properties** panel.

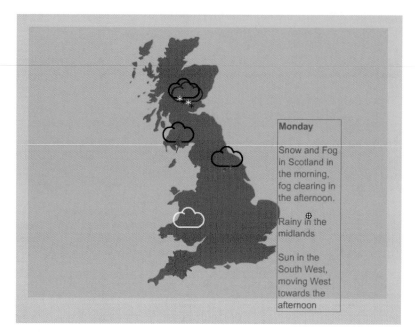

Figure 11.11: Writing the scrolling text for Monday

●   Right-click the **Monday text** layer in the **Timeline** panel and select **Insert Layer** from the menu that appears. Name this layer **Text mask**.

▢ ───●   Click the **Rectangle** tool in the **Toolbox**. Draw a rectangle that covers the first four lines of the text box. Make the rectangle slightly wider than the text box. It doesn't matter what colour it is.

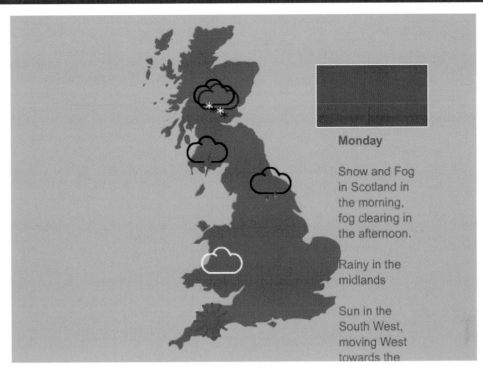

Figure 11.12: Drawing a rectangle in the Text mask layer

○ Select **Frame 100** of the **Monday text** layer. Press **F6** on the keyboard to insert a **keyframe** (this is a shortcut, it is the same as right-clicking then selecting **Insert Keyframe**).

○ Make sure that just the text is selected, and then use the **Up** arrow on the keyboard to move the **Text box** up until all the text is above the rectangle.

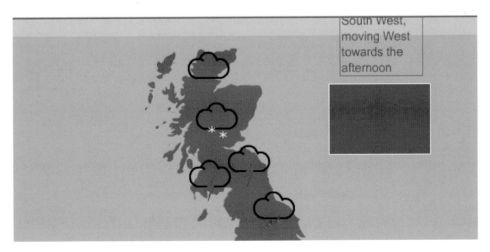

Figure 11.13: Tweening the Text box

○ Right-click any **regular frame** in the **Monday Text** layer between **Frame 1** and **Frame 100** and select **Create Motion Tween** from the menu that appears.

Have a look in the **Library** panel; notice that a library symbol called **Tween 1** (or any number) has been created.

 Rename this tween **Monday text**. Create a new folder in the **Library** panel and name it **Tweens**. Move the **Monday text** tween to the new **Tweens** folder.

Creating a Mask layer

 Now right-click the **Text mask** layer in the **Timeline** panel and select **Mask** from the list. This layer turns into a **Mask** layer, masking the layer immediately below it: in this case, the **Monday text** layer.

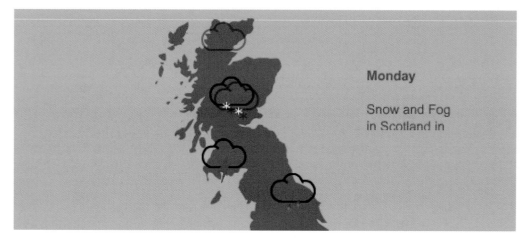

Figure 11.14

 Preview the movie by pressing **Ctrl-Enter**. The text should scroll up!

Slowing down an animation

You may find that the text moves too quickly. There are two ways in which we can slow the movie down:

❶ Edit the **frame rate**. As explained in Chapter 7, this is not good practice; you should leave the frame rate at 12 fps, which most computers can comfortably handle.

❶ Increase the number of **regular frames** between **keyframes**. This is a better way of slowing down a movie.

Inserting regular frames

We need to insert the same number of **regular frames** in all the layers. We will insert **25** more **regular frames** to increase the length of the movie to **125** frames in total.

◉ We'll insert the new frames at about **Frame 80**. Click at the top of the **Timeline** panel in **Frame 80**. You need to click above where the frames are, where the frame numbers are (see screenshot below). The red **playhead** will appear there, but no frames will actually be selected.

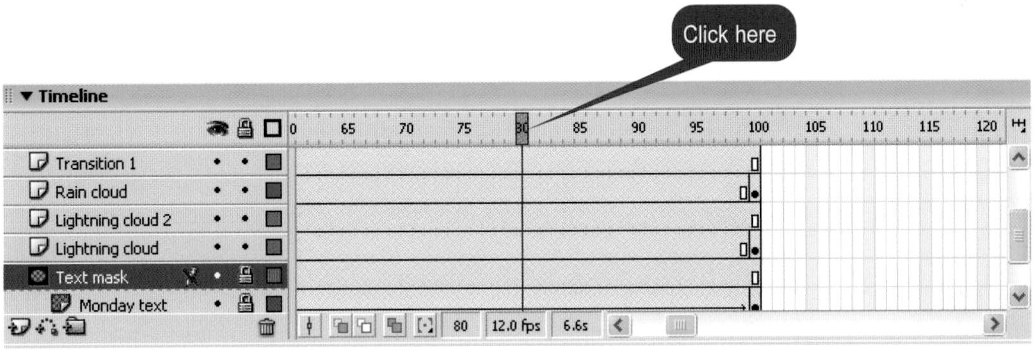

Figure 11.15: Inserting Regular frames in the Timeline panel

◉ Now press the **F5** key. This is the shortcut key to insert a **regular frame**. Notice that an extra frame has been created.

◉ Keep pressing **F5** until the total length of the movie is about **125** frames.

◉ Save the **Weather Map.fla** file, then preview the movie again (you need to press **Ctrl-Enter** again). If you're still not happy with the length of the movie, just add some more frames like you did above!

That's the Monday weather map completed.

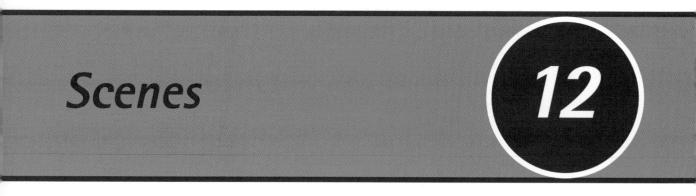

Scenes

You can split up a **Flash** movie into **scenes**. **Scenes** allow you to create the different parts of the movie separately; when published, the scenes are played one after another. We will use a different scene for each day of the week.

The Scene panel

  Open the **Weather map.fla** file.

  Select **Window**, **Design Panels**, **Scene** from the **Main Menu** bar, to display the **Scene** panel.

Dock the **Scene** panel by clicking and dragging here. Drop it under the other panels on the right of the screen

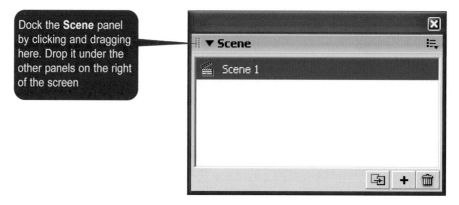

Figure 12.1: The Scene panel

Currently there is just one scene, **Scene 1**, which contains the Monday weather map.

Renaming Scenes

  Double-click in the **Scene** panel where it says **Scene 1**, and type **Monday**. Press **Enter**.

Inserting a new scene

 ❍ Select the **Monday** scene in the **Scene** panel, then click the **Duplicate** icon at the bottom of the panel.

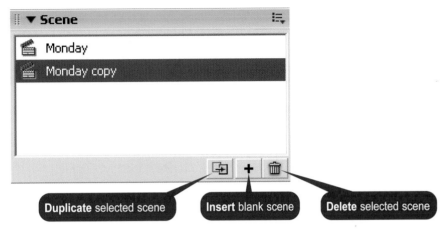

Figure 12.2: Duplicating a scene

❍ Rename the new scene **Tuesday**.

Deleting layers

We will keep the scrolling text and the background layers, but all the others need to be deleted so that we can start again, creating Tuesday's weather.

❍ Make sure **Tuesday** is selected in the **Scene** panel. Click the first layer in the **Timeline** panel. Scroll down to the last layer before the text and background layers. Hold down the **Shift** key then click the last layer you want to delete. This selects all the layers between your two selections.

 ❍ Now click the small **Delete Layer** icon at the bottom of the **Timeline** panel.

Figure 12.3: Deleting layers in the Timeline panel

The selected layers are deleted.

Editing the Text box layer

We need to edit the **Monday text** layer to contain Tuesday's weather. Because the text box is actually a symbol in the **Library** (it was added automatically because of the tween), if we change the text here, it will change the symbol and therefore change the text on the **Monday** scene too. To avoid this, we will have to copy the **Monday text** tween, then insert the copy in place of the original.

Notice that there is a padlock symbol next to the layer name. This means that the layer is locked.

Unlocking a layer

▶ We need to unlock the layer in order to be able to edit the text. To do this, just click the padlock symbol next to the **Monday text** layer name.

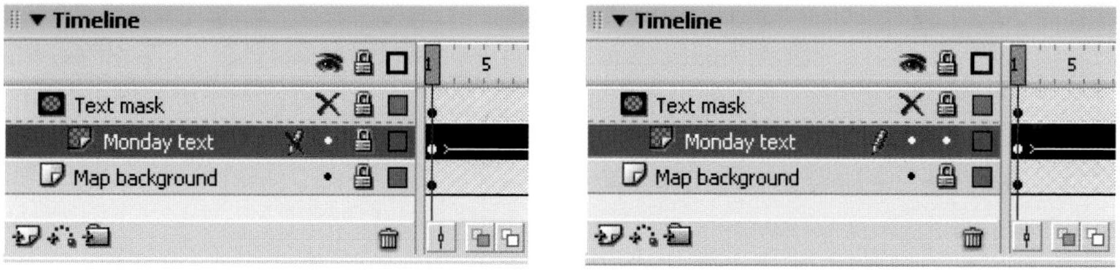

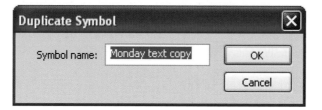

Figure 12.4: Locking a layer in the Timeline panel

▶ In the **Monday text** layer, right-click the text on the **Stage** then select **Duplicate Symbol** from the menu that appears. This will duplicate the existing tween symbol.

Figure 12.5: Duplicating a symbol

▶ Name it **Tuesday text**. Click **OK**.

○ Click in **Frame 1** of the **Monday text** layer. Now, using the **Selection** tool, double-click on the text box.

Tip: If you want to hide the **Text mask** layer, just click under the **eye** symbol next to the **Text mask** layer name in the **Timeline** panel.

This will take you into **Symbol edit** mode. Look at the top of the **Timeline** panel; notice that it now says **Tuesday text**.

| ← | 📇 Tuesday 🅱 Tuesday text | 📇 📇 100% ⌄ |

Figure 12.6: Symbol edit mode

○ Edit the text using the **Text** tool.

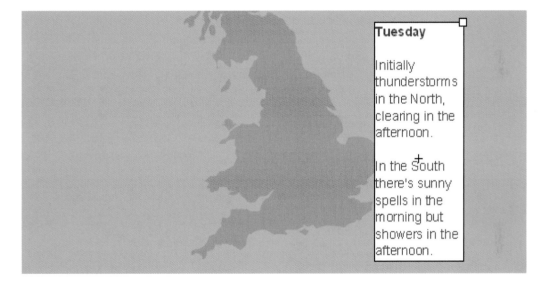

Figure 12.7

○ When you have finished editing the text, exit **Symbol edit** mode by clicking where it says **Tuesday** above the **Timeline** panel.

○ Rename the layer **Tuesday text** in the **Timeline** panel.

○ Now lock the **Tuesday text** layer by clicking under the padlock symbol in the **Timeline** panel.

Add the weather symbols

    ◉   Unlock the **Map background** layer. With **Frame 1** of the **Map background** layer selected, drag some symbols across from the **Library** panel. Remember to distribute all the symbols to layers.

    ◉   Move the **Map background** to the bottom of the list of layers.

    ◉   Lock the **Map background** layer again.

    ◉   Animate the symbols just like you did for the **Monday** scene. Try to make them match the text you have just written!

Tidying the Timeline panel

You can tidy up all your layers in the **Timeline** panel by putting all the symbol layers in a new folder.

    ◉   Click the **Insert Layer Folder** icon at the bottom of the **Timeline** panel. Name the folder **Symbols** then click and drag all the symbols and drop them onto the new folder. You can expand and collapse the new folder by clicking the small arrow icon to the left of the folder name.

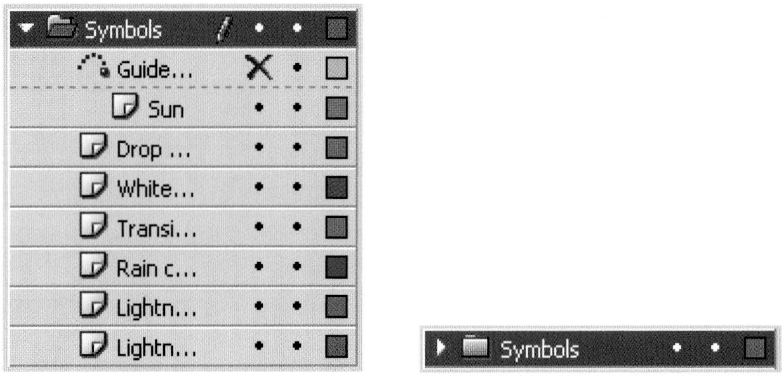

Figure 12.8: Collapsing a folder in the Timeline panel

Add an Intro scene

Before creating the other pages for all the days of the week, we'll add an initial scene called Intro.

 ● In the Scene panel, click the Monday scene, then click the Duplicate Scene icon.

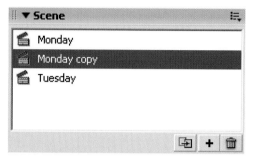

Figure 12.9: The Scene panel

● Rename the new scene Intro.

Rearranging the Scene panel

The new scene appears below the original Monday scene. The scenes will play in the order in which they appear in the Scene panel, so we need to move the Intro scene to the top of the Scene panel.

● Click and drag the Intro scene and drop it above the Monday scene at the top of the Scene panel.

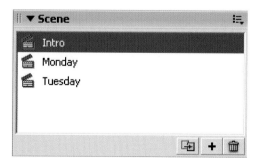

Figure 12.10: The Scene panel, reordered

Now, in the **Timeline** panel, delete all the layers except the **Map background** layer by selecting them all, then clicking the **Delete** icon at the bottom of the **Timeline** panel.

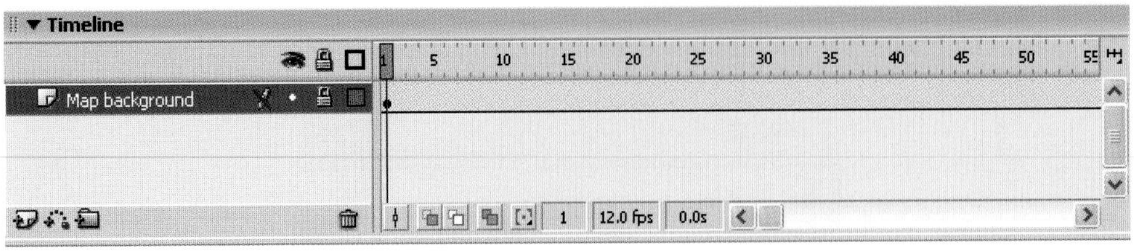

Figure 12.11: The Timeline panel

Save by pressing **Ctrl-S**.

Shape tweening

Shape tweening is similar to **motion tweening** except that you change an object's shape rather than its position. As an introduction scene, we will start with a green circle that slowly changes into the green map of Britain.

At the moment there should be two **keyframes** – one in **Frame 1** and one in **Frame 125** – both showing the map background. We will change the first **keyframe** to show only a green circle.

First unlock the **Map background** layer in the **Timeline** panel. Click in **Frame 1** of the **Map background** layer. With the **Selection** tool, click the map then press the **Delete** key.

Now click the **Oval** tool in the **Toolbox**. Draw a green circle in the middle of the **Stage**. Delete the circle outline if there is one.

Figure 12.12

Break Apart

For **shape tweening** to work, the objects need to be **broken apart**. The circle is already a **Stage level** object with no outline, and as such will not need to be broken apart. The map, however, *will* need to be broken apart.

○ Select the last **keyframe** on the **Map background** layer; this frame should show the map. Click to select the map, then choose **Modify, Break Apart** from the **Main Menu** bar.

The map should appear with a mesh of white dots on it; this means it is broken apart enough for **shape tweening**! (If the map doesn't appear with dots on it, try breaking it apart again by selecting **Modify, Break Apart** from the **Main Menu** bar.)

Figure 12.13: Breaking apart a grouped object

⦿   Now, click to select any frame between the two **keyframes**. In the **Properties** panel, where it says **Tween**, select **Shape** from the list.

▼ Properties				
Frame	Tween:	Shape	Sound:	None
<Frame Label>	Ease:	0	Effect:	None Edit...
Label type: Name	Blend:	Distributive	Sync:	Event Repeat 1
				No sound selected.

Figure 12.14: The Properties panel showing frame properties

○ Preview the tween by pressing **Ctrl-Enter**.

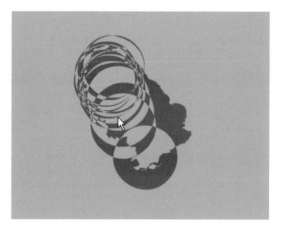

Figure 12.15: A messy Shape Tween

The tween works, but it looks a bit messy. This is because of all the islands; it is best to have just one shape when using a tween otherwise the results can be a bit unexpected. We need to delete the islands for the duration of the tween.

○ Right-click on the tween line in the **Timeline** panel, then select **Remove Tween** from the menu that appears.

○ Convert the frame just before the last **keyframe (Frame 124)** into a **keyframe** by clicking it and then pressing **F6**.

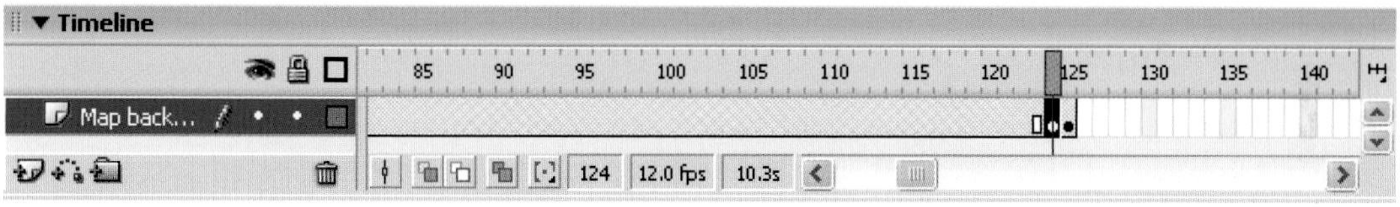

Figure 12.16: The Timeline panel

○ Delete the circle by selecting it then pressing the **Delete** key.

○ In the last frame (containing the map), deselect everything, then click the main part of the map to select it; don't select any of the islands. Choose **Edit, Copy** from the **Main Menu** bar.

◉   Click in **Frame 124**. Select **Edit, Paste in Place** from the **Main Menu** bar.

Figure 12.17: The British map with no islands

The map is pasted without the islands!

◉   Now click in a frame between **1** and **124**, then in the **Properties** panel select **Shape** from the **Tween** menu.

◉   Press **Ctrl-Enter** to preview the tween. Try experimenting with the **Ease** and **Blend** options in the **Properties** panel (make sure you have a frame selected first).

Shape Hints

If the tween doesn't move exactly as you want it to, you can add one or more shape hints.

◉   Select the circle in **Frame 1**. Choose **Modify, Shape, Add Shape Hint** from the menu.

A small red circle appears.

◉ Click and drag the red circle to the edge of the green circle, as shown below. Now go to **Frame 124** and click and drag the shape hint on the map to the position shown below.

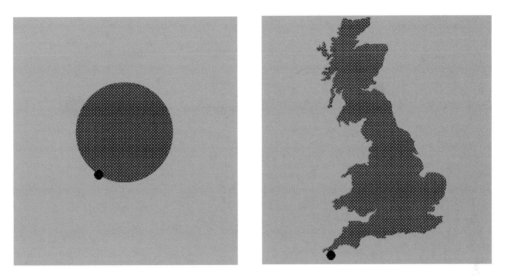

Figure 12.18: Positioning shape hints

◉ Try previewing the tween again. Is it any better? You can add more shape hints using the same method if you need to.

> **Tip:** To remove a shape hint, right-click it then select **Remove Hint** from the menu that appears.

◉ If you want the tween to move a bit quicker, remove about 40 of the **regular frames** in the middle of the tween, thus reducing the total number of frames in the **Intro** scene. (Drag across the frames in the timeline to select them, then right-click and select **Remove frames**.)

> **Tip:** If your shape hints disappear then **Flash** has probably hidden them. To unhide them select **View, Show Shape Hints** from the **Main Menu** bar.

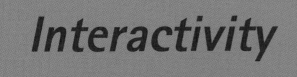

Interactivity

Now we're going to add some interactivity to the **Weather map** movie. We will create some buttons on the **Intro** scene that allow people to choose which day of the week to view. At the end of each day the movie will return to the **Intro** scene, rather than just playing through all the scenes sequentially.

Frame labels

Before we start using behaviours, we will name the frames that we want to refer to. The alternative to naming frames is just to say which frame number you are referring to, but if you add or delete frames whilst editing your movie then all your references to frame numbers will probably become wrong. The best practice is always to name frames.

○ In the **Scene** panel, select **Monday**. Right-click the first layer in the **Timeline** panel and select **Insert Layer** from the menu that appears. Rename the new layer **Actions**.

○ Click in **Frame 1** in the **Actions** layer. In the **Properties** panel, in the top-left corner where it says <Frame Label>, enter **mon**.

Figure 13.1: The Properties panel showing frame properties

○ Repeat this for the **Tuesday** scene: Insert a layer called **Actions** and name the first frame **tues**. If you've done the other days of the week, repeat this for those too.

○ In the **Intro** scene, insert an **Actions** layer at the top of the **Timeline** panel and name the first frame **intro_start**.

○ Insert a **keyframe** into the same frame of the new **Actions** layer as the final **keyframe** in the **Map background** layer. Name it **intro_menu**.

> **Tip:** You cannot name a **regular frame**. If you try to name a **regular frame**, the name will actually be attached to the preceding **keyframe**. If you want to name a frame, make it a **keyframe** first.

Adding buttons

We'll make a very simple button that will then be duplicated and used as the basis for all the other buttons.

 In the **Intro** scene, insert another layer – called **Buttons** – above the **Map background** layer.

 Select the last frame of the **Buttons** layer (this should be the same as the last frame of the **Map background** layer) then press **F6** to convert it to a **keyframe**.

 Select the **Rectangle** tool in the **Toolbox**. If you can't see the tool properties in the Properties panel, click once anywhere on the **Stage**. Set the properties to a green fill and no stroke. Drag out a small rectangle without a border, as shown below.

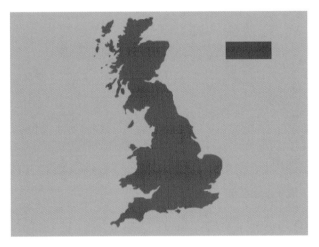

Figure 13.2

Creating a button symbol

 Select the rectangle with the **Selection** tool, then choose **Modify, Convert to Symbol** from the **Main Menu** bar.

 Enter the settings as shown below, then click **OK**.

Figure 13.3

The **GreenButton** symbol will be added to the **Library** panel.

Editing a button

○   In the **Library** panel, click the **GreenButton** once, then double-click the **GreenButton** symbol in the preview window of the **Library** panel.

Figure 13.4: The Library panel

You have now entered **Button edit** mode.

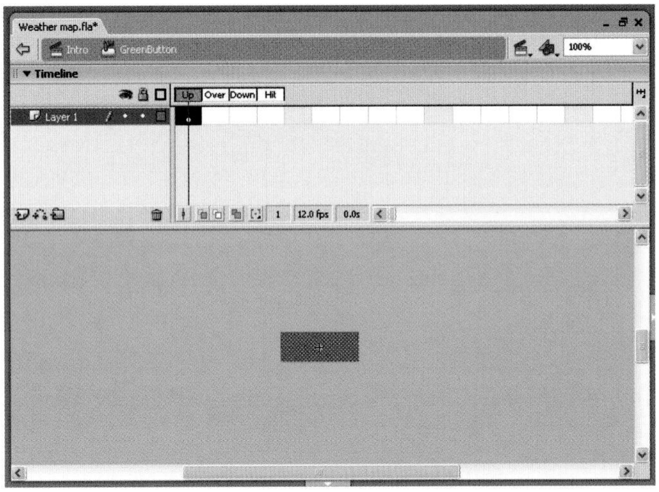

Figure 13.5: Button edit mode

Look at the **Timeline** panel. The frames have been replaced with **Up**, **Over**, **Down** and **Hit**. This is because when we created the symbol we specified the symbol type as **Button**.

The four frames represent what the button will look like in each state.

○   Convert each of the four frames into a **keyframe**. Change the colour of the button for each frame by clicking in each frame then changing the fill colour in the **Properties** panel. You can even change the shape of the button in one of the frames if you like – try using the **Free Transform** tool to make the button a bit bigger (hold down the **Alt** key so that the centre of the shape doesn't move whilst resizing).

Tip: There are loads of much more exciting button effects you can create; you can draw a different shape in one of the frames – experiment a bit!

 ○ When you've finished editing the button, click where it says **Intro** above the **Timeline** panel to exit **Button edit** mode.

Figure 13.6

 ○ Drag out another couple of instances of the **GreenButton** onto the **Stage**. Deliberately misalign them as shown in Figure 13.7.

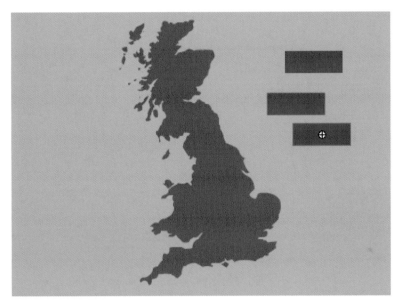

Figure 13.7: Deliberately misaligned buttons

The Align panel

We'll use the **Align** panel to line up the buttons.

○   If you can't see the **Align** panel, select **Window, Design Panels, Align** from the **Main Menu** bar.

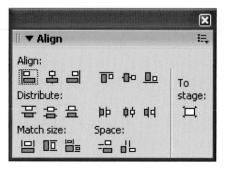

Figure 13.8: The Align panel

○   Select all three buttons by holding down the **Shift** key while you click them with the **Selection** tool.

○   Now click the top-left icon to align the left edges of the buttons. You can also even out the spaces between the buttons by clicking the left-hand **Space** icon.

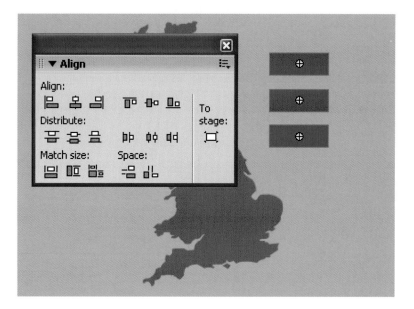

Figure 13.9: Aligning the buttons using the Align panel

The buttons are now neatly positioned!

○   Close the **Align** panel by clicking the red **Close** icon at the top right of the panel.

○   Press **Ctrl-S** to save.

Adding Behaviours

Any sort of interactivity in **Flash** is written in **ActionScript**. If you want to do some of the more advanced things in **Flash** then you'll probably end up learning some **ActionScript** programming. However, you'll be pleased to hear that we'll be using the **Behaviours** panel to write most of the **ActionScript** for us!

◉   First use the **Text** tool to write some labels on the buttons, as shown in Figure 13.10.

◉   If you find that the text gets hidden behind a button, first make sure that you're not in **Button edit** mode – if you are, **GreenButton** will be written above the **Timeline** panel alongside where it says **Intro** (to exit **Button edit** mode, just click where it says **Intro** above the **Timeline** panel). If the text is still hidden, right-click the button, then select **Arrange**, **Send to Back** from the menu that appears.

Figure 13.10

The Stop action

The first action we will add is to stop the **Intro** scene at the last frame, where the buttons appear. If we don't do this, the movie will just carry on, and the **Monday** scene will be played immediately after the **Intro** scene. The buttons would only be visible for one short frame!

The **Stop** action will be put in the **Actions** layer of the **Intro** scene, in the **keyframe** labelled **intro_menu**.

The Actions and Behaviors panels

We need both the **Actions** panel and the **Behaviors** panel open.

- Select **Window, Development Panels, Actions** to open the **Actions** panel.
- Select **Window, Development Panels, Behaviors** to open the **Behaviors** panel.

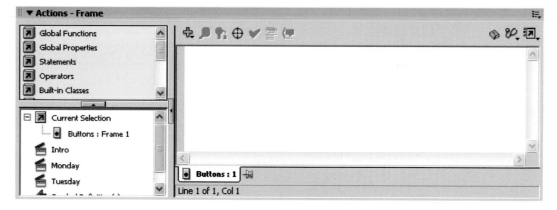

Figure 13.11: The Actions panel

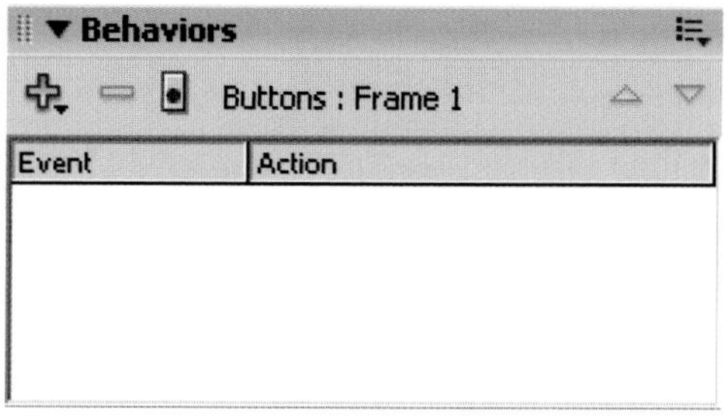

Figure 13.12: The Behaviors panel

- Now click to select the last **keyframe** in the **Actions** layer of the **Intro** scene. This frame should already be named **intro_menu**.

For the **Stop** action, we won't use the **Behaviours** panel, because adding it manually is so straightforward.

◉   In the **Actions** panel, simply type **stop()**. That's your first taste of **ActionScript**!

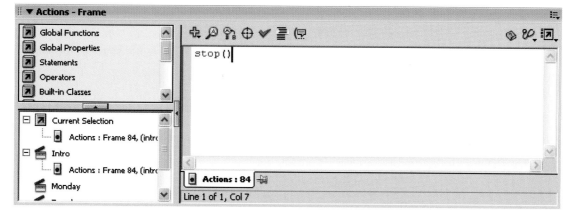

Figure 13.13: The Actions panel

◉   Play the movie by pressing **Ctrl-Enter**. The movie should stop at the end of the **Intro** scene, rather than going straight onto the **Monday** scene.

Adding actions to buttons

At the moment the buttons don't do anything because we haven't assigned any actions to them. To add actions we'll use the **Behaviors** panel. The action we will use is the **Goto and Play** action; this is a very popular action, which does just as it says – goes to a frame and plays the movie!

◉   Click on the second button, marked **Monday**, to select it. Be careful to select the button and not the text. Make sure that you aren't in **Button edit** mode – if you are, **GreenButton** will be written above the **Timeline** panel alongside where it says **Intro**. To exit **Button edit** mode, just click where it says **Intro**.

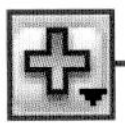

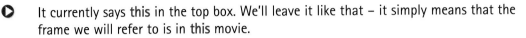 In the **Behaviors** panel, click the small **+** symbol at the top left of the panel to add a behaviour. Select **Movieclip** then **Goto and Play at frame or label** from the menu that appears.

> It currently says **this** in the top box. We'll leave it like that – it simply means that the frame we will refer to is in **this** movie.

> Make sure **Relative** is selected. In the last box, where it currently says **1**, type **mon**. This is the frame we want to start playing at. Click **OK**.

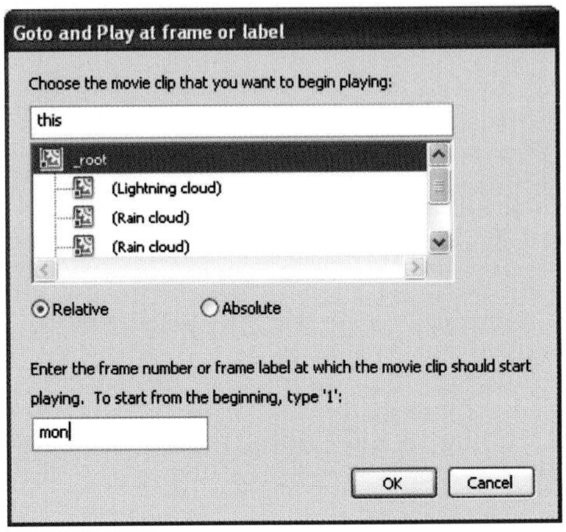

Figure 13.14: The Goto and Play behaviour

Now look at the **Actions** panel. The **Behaviors** panel has written the **gotoAndPlay** code for you. If you were more familiar with **ActionScript** you could have just typed in this code without using the **Behaviors** panel.

Notice the **on (release)** line. Actions can only be attached to a button when you specify what will start the action. **On (release)** is the standard for buttons; this means that the action will happen when the button is released. Other possible commands would be **on (click)** or **on (over)** – there are plenty more!

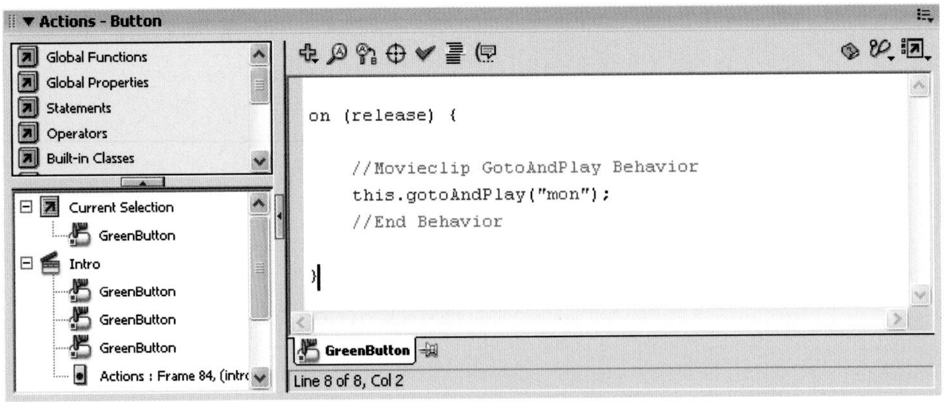

```
on (release) {

        //Movieclip GotoAndPlay Behavior
        this.gotoAndPlay("mon");
        //End Behavior

}
```

Figure 13.15: The Actions panel

Test it!

○   Press **Ctrl-Enter** to play the **Intro** scene. Click the **Monday** button and see what happens!

The **Monday** scene should play. The **Tuesday** scene will play after the **Monday** scene – we'll change that in a moment.

○   Now add the code for the **Tuesday** button using the same method. Remember, this time you need to enter **tues** as the frame label in the **Goto and Play** window. Test the **Tuesday** button.

○   Add a **gotoAndPlay** action to the **Intro** button that plays the movie at the start of the **Intro** scene, at the **intro_start** frame label.

Returning to the Intro menu

We need to add the actions that return the movie to the **Intro menu** (that is, the **intro_menu** frame in the **Intro** scene) after playing each scene. To do this we will add a **gotoAndPlay** action that goes to the **intro_menu** label to the last frame in each scene.

○   Click the last frame in the **Actions** layer in the **Monday** scene. Make it a **keyframe** if it is not already.

 ──○   In the **Behaviors** panel, click the + symbol to add a behaviour. Again, select **Movieclip, Goto and Play at frame or label** from the menu that appears.

○   In the **Goto and Play** window, enter **intro_menu** as the frame label. Click **OK**.

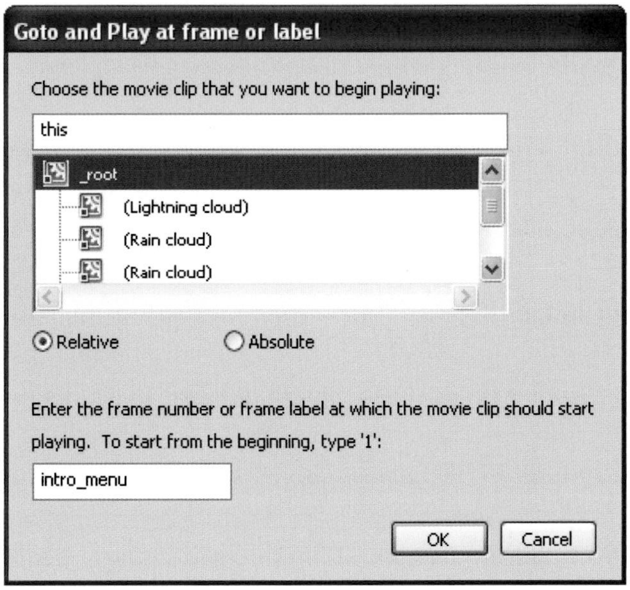

Figure 13.16: The Goto and Play behaviour

◉   Take a look at the code in the **Actions** panel.

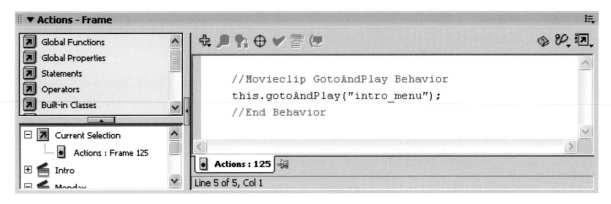

```
//Movieclip GotoAndPlay Behavior
this.gotoAndPlay("intro_menu");
//End Behavior
```

Figure 13.17: The Actions panel

The code is almost identical to the code attached to the button, except this time, because it is a frame not a button, there is no **on (release)** line.

◉   Add the same **gotoAndPlay** action at the end of the **Tuesday** scene, and any other days if you've created them. Remember that you must convert a frame into a **keyframe** in order to add an action to it. Only add actions to the **Action** layers you have created.

◉   Preview the movie by pressing **Ctrl-Enter**. Test the movie by clicking all the buttons and making sure they do what they are supposed to.

◉   Save the movie, then close **Flash** if this is the end of a session.

Adding Sound

14

There are two types of sound we will use in this movie:

The first type is an **event sound**. The sound is played as a result of an action, such as the user clicking a button. A sound event is completely downloaded by the user's computer before being played, and is played in full once the event has been triggered, regardless of any other actions that occur during the sound.

The second type is a **streaming sound** that is synchronized with the movie. A streaming sound is a sound that is downloaded as it is being played. This is particularly useful for a large sound file; without streaming, the user would have to wait until the whole sound file had been downloaded before being able to listen to it. With streaming, only a small section of the file need be downloaded before the sound starts playing. A streaming sound can be stopped before the whole file is played.

Compatible File Types

There are three sound types that can be imported into **Flash**:

- ❶ **.wav** (Windows)
- ❶ **.aiff** (Mac)
- ❶ **MP3** (Windows and Mac)

Downloading sounds

There are plenty of websites where you can download free sounds – try just typing **free sound effects** into **Google** and seeing what comes up.

One website that has free sounds is **Wav Central**.

●   Go to www.wavcentral.com.

Tip: Another good site that has free sounds and sound effects is **www.findsounds.com**

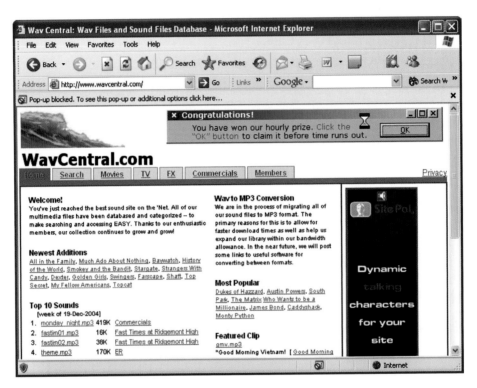

Figure 14.1: The Wav Central website

●   Click the **Search** tab at the top of the page, then type **thunder** in the search box and click the **Search** button.

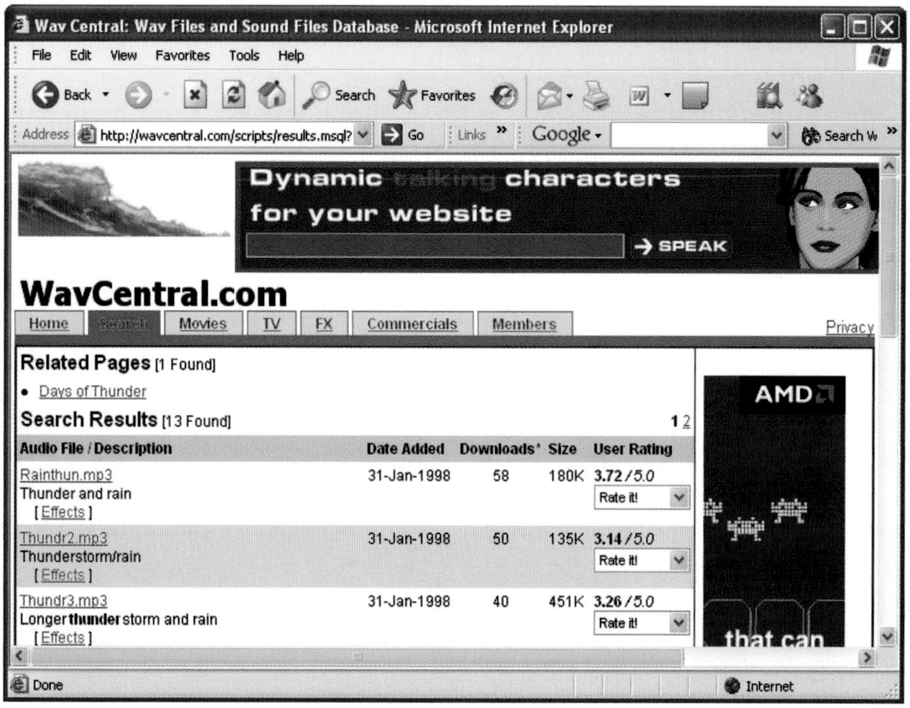

Figure 14.2: The Wav Central website

There are a few different thunder sounds here!

◐ To listen to the sounds, just click them once. Windows Media Player will load and then play the sound clip.

◐ Find a medium-length thunder clip: about 150 K in size will do. Right-click the file name then select Save Target As from the menu that appears.

Figure 14.3: Right-clicking a sound file

◐ Create a Sounds folder in the Weather Project folder. Save the file as thunder.

Notice that the file type is **MP3** – this is fine, as **MP3s** are supported by **Flash**. Click **Save**.

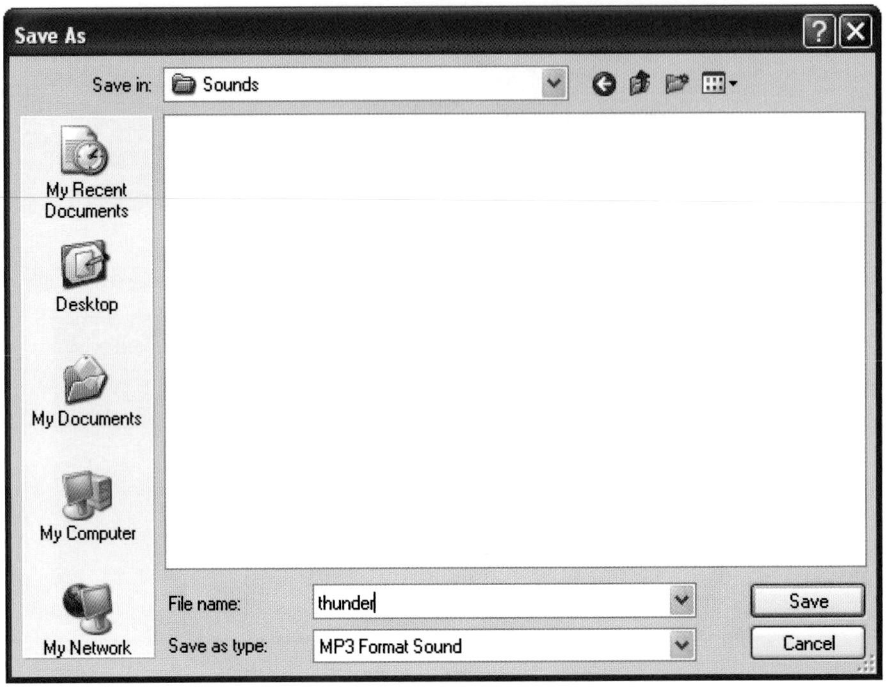

Figure 14.4: The Save As window

Recording your own sounds

You can record your own sounds using **Windows Sound Recorder**, which you've probably got on your computer.

◐   To open **Windows Sound Recorder** click the **Start** button at the bottom-left of your screen. Select **All Programs**, **Accessories**, **Entertainment**, **Sound Recorder** from the menu.

◐   Record a sound then save it in the **Sounds** folder.

Tip: For more detailed information about how to record your own sounds go to **www.paynegallway.co.uk/flash**.

Importing sounds

- Open **Flash** if it's not already open, and load the **Weather map** file.

- Select **File, Import, Import to Library** from the **Main Menu** bar.

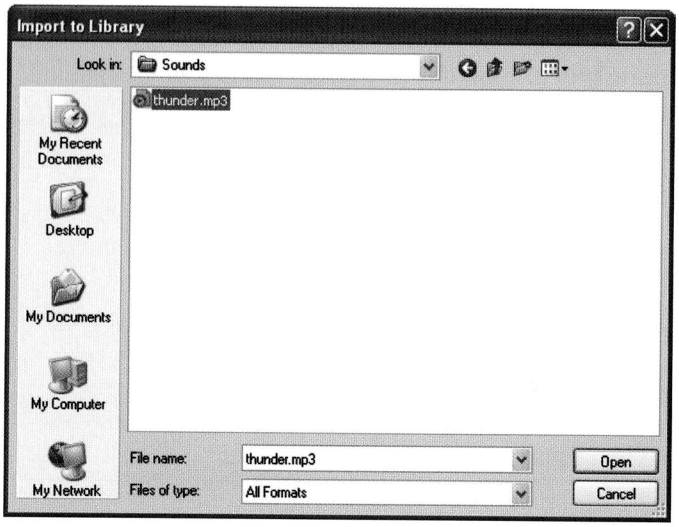

Figure 14.5: Importing a sound file to the Library

- Find the **thunder.mp3** file in the **Sounds** folder, then click **Open**.

We'll create a separate folder in the **Library** panel to put sounds in.

- At the bottom of the **Library** panel, click the **Add New Folder** icon. Name the folder **Sounds**.

- Scroll down the **Library** panel to find the new sound file that you have just imported. Click and drag the new file and drop it onto the **Sounds** folder.

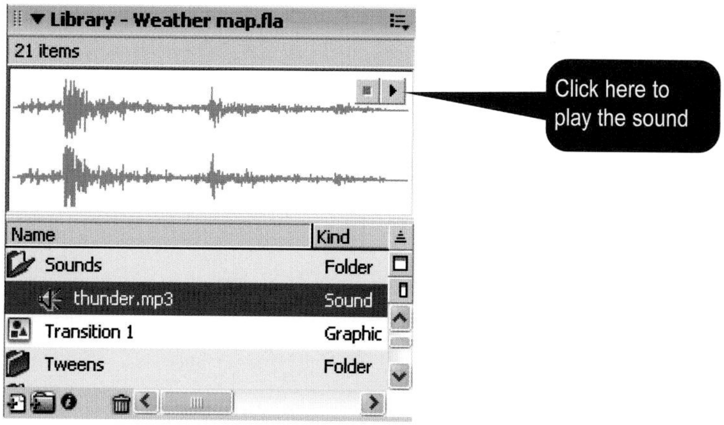

Figure 14.6: The sound files are shown in the Library

Notice that the preview window shows a visual representation of the sound.

143

Playing a sound in Flash

▶ Click to select the sound in the **Library** panel, then click the small **Play** icon at the top-right of the panel in the **Preview** window.

Inserting a sound into a movie

We'll attach the thunder sound to the **Monday** weather map.

▶ Select the **Monday** scene by clicking it in the **Scene** panel. Insert a new layer and name it **Sounds**. Select the first frame in the new **Sounds** layer.

▶ Click and drag the **thunder.mp3** file from the **Library** panel and drop it anywhere on the **Stage**.

The sound is inserted into the new layer!

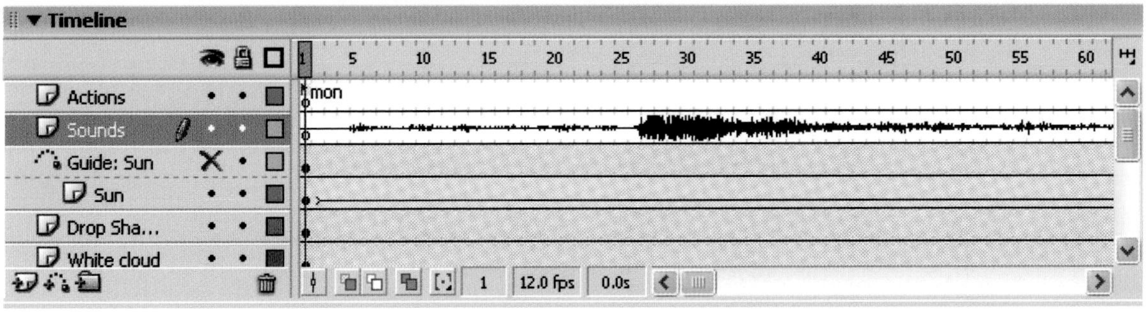

Figure 14.7: Sounds layer in the Timeline panel

▶ Preview the movie by pressing **Ctrl-Enter**. Click the **Monday** button to listen to the new sound.

Event sound vs. Streaming sound

This works, but the sound is longer than the **Monday** scene, so it carries on playing even when the **Monday** scene has finished. This is because, at the moment, it is an **event sound**. If we made it a **streaming sound**, it would remain synchronised with the movie, and would stop playing when the **Monday** scene ended.

 Select **Frame 1** in the **Sounds** layer. In the **Properties** panel, click the down-arrow where it says **Sync**, then select **Stream** from the list.

 Preview the movie again to see if that works.

Sounds placed in **keyframes** can either be **event** or **stream** sounds. It is actually better to use **event sounds** where possible because they have the least impact on performance. Sometimes with **stream sounds**, the visual parts of a movie will be sacrificed if the computer can't keep up, in an effort to maintain synchronisation.

We'll now look at how to keep the sound as an **event sound** by editing the sound to be the same length as the **Monday** scene.

Editing a sound

 Select **Frame 1** in the **Sounds** layer. In the **Properties** panel, first reselect **Event** as the **Sync** option. Now click the **Edit** button on the right.

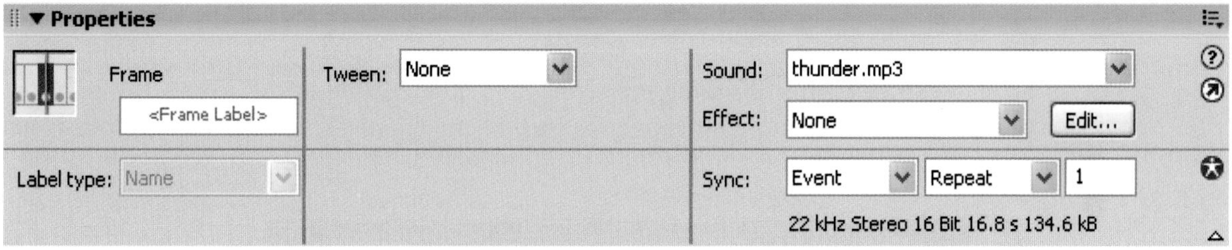

Figure 14.8: The Properties panel showing Frame properties

The **Edit Envelope** window appears. The two lines represent the two channels of the sound: one left, one right.

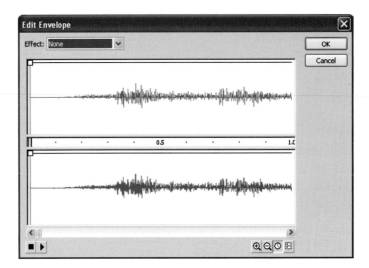

Figure 14.9: The Edit Envelope window

At the moment, the sound length is being displayed in **seconds**. It would be more useful to us if it was in **frames**.

○ In the bottom-right of the window, click the **Frames** icon.

We'll fade the sound out at about **Frame 120**.

○ Scroll along to **Frame 120** using the scroll bar at the bottom of the screen. Notice that there is a thin black line running above each of the channels. Click this line above **Frame 120**.

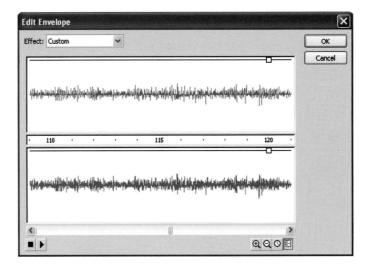

Figure 14.10: The Edit Envelope window

A small node appears on the line.

○ Click the line again at **Frame 110** to add a second node. Now click and drag the node at **Frame 120** down to the bottom of the wave. Do this for both channels.

Tip: If you make a mistake and want to start again, select **None** from the menu at the top of the window. You can also try some of the other effects listed here!

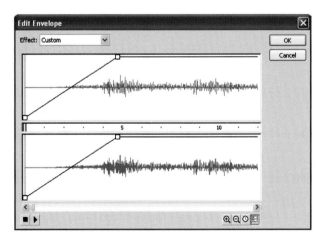

Figure 14.11: Fading a sound out using the Edit Envelope window

This will effectively fade out the sound between **Frame 110** and **Frame 120**.

○ You can also fade a sound in by adding a couple of nodes at **Frame 1** and **Frame 10** then dragging the node at **Frame 1** down to the bottom axis.

Tip: Always edit both the channels equally. If you don't, you'll find that one speaker is louder than the other.

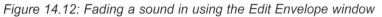

Figure 14.12: Fading a sound in using the Edit Envelope window

○ Click **OK** when you're finished.

○ Preview the movie again to see if it works.

Attaching a sound to a button

As well as placing sounds in **keyframes** on the timeline, you can also add a sound event to a button so that it plays when the button is clicked. We'll attach a short sound to play when a button is pressed.

⊙   First of all, download or record a suitable button noise, then import it into your **Flash** movie so that it is in the **Sounds** folder in the **Library**.

⊙   In the **Library** panel, double-click the **GreenButton** to edit it.

⊙   Add a **keyframe** to the **Hit** frame if there isn't one already. Select the **keyframe** then click and drag the new button noise onto the **Stage**.

⊙   With the **Hit** frame selected, change the **Sync** option in the **Properties** panel to **Event** (if it isn't already). If this option is set to **Stream**, the sound won't play, because the scene finishes as soon as the button is pressed, and a **Stream** sound will finish with the scene.

⊙   Save the movie and then test it.

Publishing Options 15

HTML and .swf files

We have already looked at how to publish a movie to create an **HTML** file and a **Flash Player SWF** file. To view either of these files, extra software is required by the user. For the **HTML** file you need to have a web browser and a copy of **Flash Player** (which can be downloaded free). For an **FLA** file you just need **Flash Player**.

Projector files

It is possible to publish your **Flash** movie so that it is a stand-alone application. It can be played on any computer, as everything needed to run the movie is contained in the file. These stand-alone files are called **Projector** files. These are very useful because they can be played straight from a CD-ROM, floppy disk, or hard drive.

 Select **File**, **Publish Settings** from the **Main Menu** bar.

● Under the **Formats** tab, click to select **Windows Projector (.exe)**. Also leave the **Flash** and **HTML** options ticked.

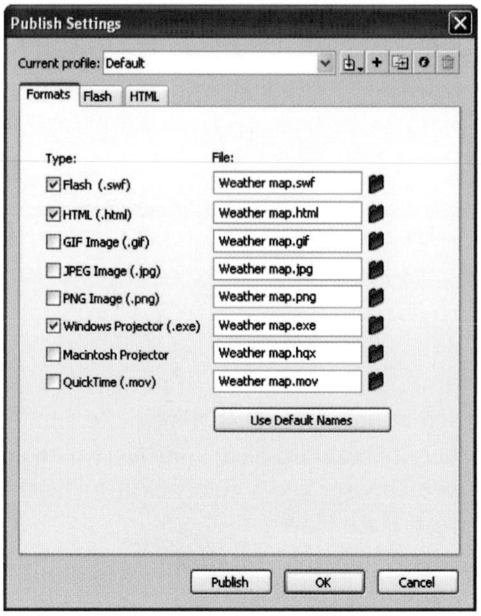

Figure 15.1: The Publish Settings window

Usually, for each of the options you tick, a new tab appears with options for that file type. With **Projector** files this doesn't happen – you don't get any options! That makes things a bit simpler.

● Click **Publish**, then click **OK**.

● Open **Windows Explorer** and look for the new file **Weather map.exe** in the **Weather Project** folder.

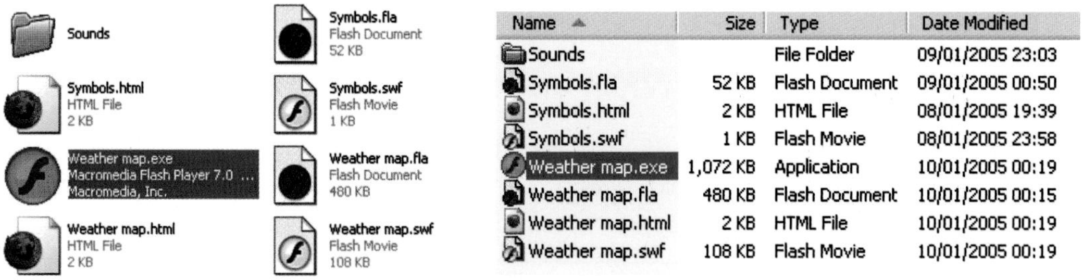

Figure 15.2: Finding the Projector (.exe) file in Windows Explorer

● To run this application, just double-click the file in **Windows Explorer**.

Figure 15.3: Running the Projector file

The application starts playing! It will play exactly the same on a computer that doesn't have **Flash**.

Inserting a Flash movie into a Dreamweaver web page

If you have used **Dreamweaver**, you'll find it useful to know how to insert a **Flash** movie into an **HTML** page using **Dreamweaver**.

● Open **Dreamweaver**. Either open a website that you have already created, or create a new one.

● Create a new **HTML** page; you can either create a blank page or base it on a template – it depends how you want the page to look, and if it is part of a larger site.

● Place the mouse pointer where you want the **Flash** movie to be inserted, then select **Insert, Media, Flash** from the **Main Menu** bar.

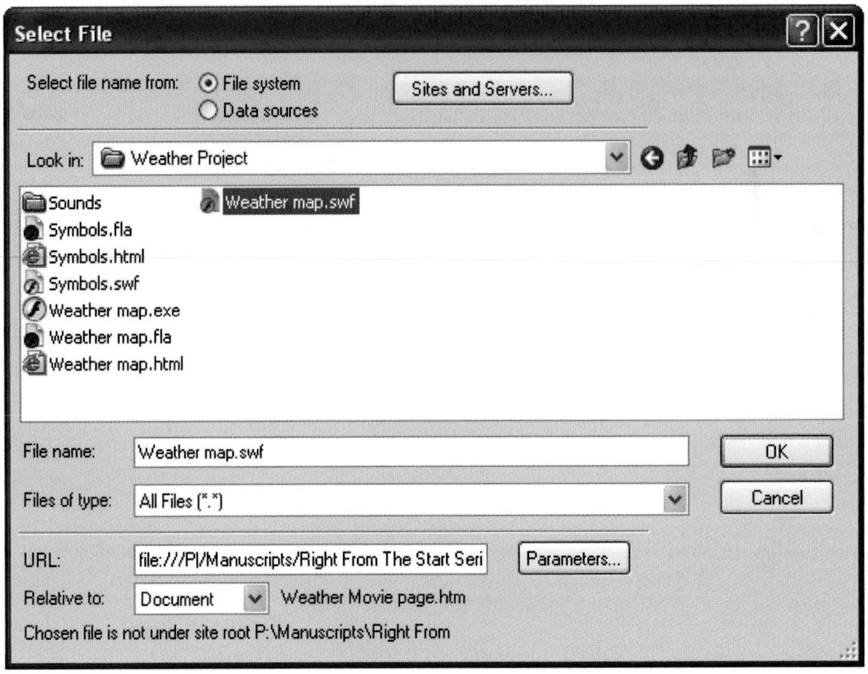

Figure 15.4: Selecting a Flash file to insert into a Dreamweaver page

◉ Find the **Flash** movie (**.swf**) file (the one with the small blue **f** icon next to it) then click **OK**.

You will get the following message:

Figure 15.5

◉ Click **Yes**. This will make a copy of the **Flash** file and store it in the root folder of your website. Select exactly where you want to store the **Flash** file – you may want to create a new folder for imported **Flash** files. Click **Save**.

The **Flash** movie appears as a large grey rectangle with an **f** icon in the middle. If you preview the page in a browser (by pressing **F12**) you will see the **Flash** movie running!

Figure 15.6: A Flash file in a Dreamweaver page

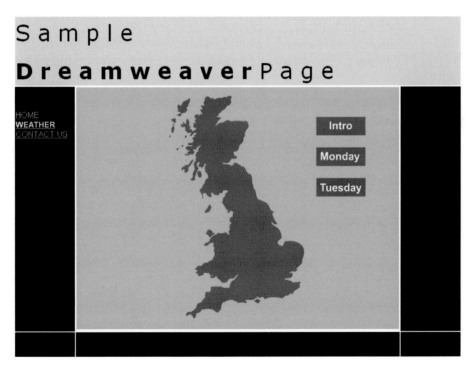

Figure 15.7: The same Dreamweaver page previewed in Internet Explorer

Improving your movie

There are loads of things you can do to make your movie even better. If you've finished the book and are looking for more ideas for exercises, try some of these!

- ❶ Insert a pause at the start of each scene. To do this, add about **10 frames** to the start of all the layers, then click and drag the first **keyframe** in the **Map background** layer back to **Frame 1**. This will display the map for a few seconds before anything happens.

- ❶ Insert some text to the **Intro** scene saying more about the weather map. Add a large title, then try breaking the title apart (**Modify, Break Apart**) and distribute all the letters to different layers. You could then tween the letters so that they break off in different directions.

- ❶ Spend some more time making the buttons look a bit more professional. Take a look at the built-in buttons **Flash** has, by selecting **Window, Other Panels, Common Libraries, Buttons**. A **Library-Buttons** panel will open with lots of different buttons.

- ❶ You can add some tweened animation to a button (to have it slowly change colour or shape when the mouse is over it). Do this by inserting a movie clip symbol based on the button into the **Over** frame of the original button.

  - ◉ To do this, first create the button, and make it a **Button** symbol. Then duplicate the **Button** symbol and make it a **Movie Clip** symbol. Make this movie about **15 frames** long, with a gradual colour change or shape tween. Now go back and edit the **Button** symbol in **Button edit** mode. Click the **Over** frame, then click and drag the button **Movieclip** symbol from the **Library** onto the **Stage**. Make sure it lines up with the button shown in the other frames (**Onion skinning** might help with this).

- ❶ How about adding some pressure lines to the map? Each line would have to be on a different layer, and you could use a **Shape Tween** to change the shape and location of the lines between the start and the end of the scene.

To view the **Weather map** movie that I created, go to the Payne-Gallway website at www.payne-gallway.co.uk/flash

Index